A Memorandum on Intrafaith Harmony in Islam

Shaykh Ḥaydar Muḥammad
Kāmil Ḥubbullāh

AL-BURĀQ

Copyright

ISBN: 978-1-956276-24-4
Printed and published by al-Burāq Publications.
Translated Dr. Muḥammad Jaffer. Edited by Sayyid ʿAlī ʿImrān. Where needed, context and transliterations were added. Some minor edits were made to the translated Arabic text.

Ordering Information
We offer discounts and promotions for wholesale purchases, non-profit organizations, and other educational institutions. Contact us at the email below for further information.

www.al-Buraq.org
publications@al-Buraq.org
First Edition | December 2022

Dedication

The publication of this book was made possible through the generous support of our donors.

بِسْمِ اللَّهِ الرَّحْمَٰنِ الرَّحِيمِ
الْحَمْدُ لِلَّهِ رَبِّ الْعَالَمِينَ الرَّحْمَٰنِ الرَّحِيمِ
مَالِكِ يَوْمِ الدِّينِ إِيَّاكَ نَعْبُدُ وَإِيَّاكَ نَسْتَعِينُ
اهْدِنَا الصِّرَاطَ الْمُسْتَقِيمَ صِرَاطَ الَّذِينَ
أَنْعَمْتَ عَلَيْهِمْ غَيْرِ الْمَغْضُوبِ عَلَيْهِمْ
وَلَا الضَّالِّينَ

Please recite *Sūrat al-Fātihah* and ask God for the Divine reward (*thawāb*) to be conferred upon the donors and also the souls of all the deceased in whose memory their loved ones have contributed graciously towards the publication of *A Memorandum on Intrafaith Harmony in Islam.*

Duʿāʾ al-Ḥujjah

اللَّهُمَّ كُنْ لِوَلِيِّكَ الْحُجَّةِ ابْنِ الْحَسَنِ صَلَوَاتُكَ
عَلَيْهِ وَعَلَى آبَائِهِ فِي هَذِهِ السَّاعَةِ وَفِي كُلِّ
سَاعَةٍ وَلِيّاً وَحَافِظاً وَقَائِداً وَنَاصِراً وَدَلِيلاً
وَعَيْناً حَتَّى تُسْكِنَهُ أَرْضَكَ طَوْعاً وَتُمَتِّعَهُ فِيهَا طَوِيلاً

O God, be, for Your representative, the Ḥujjat (proof), son of al-Ḥasan, Your blessings be upon him and his forefathers, in this hour and in every hour: a guardian, a protector, a leader, a helper, a proof, and an eye - until You make him live on the Earth, in obedience (to You), and cause him to live in it for a long time.

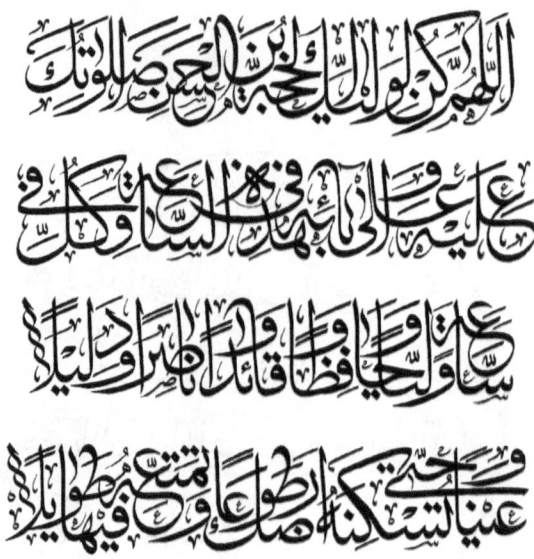

Table of Contents

Managing Our Differences: Principles, Methods, and Hermeneutics 191

What are the Necessary Steps to Take? 209

Introduction

بسم الله الرحمن الرحيم

In the Name of God, the Beneficent, the Merciful

Since the dawn of Islam, the Muslims had congregated around their Prophet ﷺ to garner from him religious instruction and learn from the Divine inspiration which descended upon him. Along with the Divine Providence and the Muḥammadan grace, the message of Islam was forged by the efforts of these individuals surrounding the Prophet ﷺ. The Muslim congregation was notably small in its size—an oppressed minority—facing all forms of oppression, tyranny, and transgression. Nonetheless it maintained its consolidation, with individuals mutually working together to embody the epitome of self-actualization, inter-cooperation, and collaboration—all in the spirit of brotherhood: a brotherhood which indeed left its impressions on the destiny of Islamic proselytization and crystallized the principles of unity and accommodation between Muslims until today; a brotherhood which emerged from individuals who had not long before been in the throes of conflict and discord.

As God ﷻ Himself states in the Qurʾān:

﴿هُوَ الَّذِي أَيَّدَكَ بِنَصْرِهِ وَبِالْمُؤْمِنِينَ﴾

huwa lladhī ʾayyadaka bi-naṣrihī wa-bi-l-muʾminīn[a]

﴿وَأَلَّفَ بَيْنَ قُلُوبِهِمْ ۚ لَوْ أَنفَقْتَ مَا فِي الْأَرْضِ جَمِيعًا مَّا أَلَّفْتَ بَيْنَ قُلُوبِهِمْ
وَلَٰكِنَّ اللَّهَ أَلَّفَ بَيْنَهُمْ ۚ إِنَّهُ عَزِيزٌ حَكِيمٌ﴾

﴿*wa-ʾallafa bayna qulūbihim law ʾanfaqta mā fī l-ʾarḍi jamīʿan mā ʾallafta bayna qulūbihim wa-lākinna llāha ʾallafa baynahum ʾinnahū ʿazīzun ḥakīm*[un]﴾

﴿*It is He who strengthened* you *with His help and with the means of the faithful, and united their hearts. Had* you *spent all that is in the earth,* you *could not have united their hearts, but God united them together. Indeed He is all-mighty, all-wise.*﴾[1]

This harmony was in the wake of Islam's values and teachings, which found their way into the hearts and souls of the Muslims to create a new generation: one that would not take long to transform the face of the world in a relatively short period of time. It was natural for some personal or impersonal dissidence to arise here and there between the Muslims, although the presence

---

[1] Sūrat al-Anfāl, Verses 62-63.

of the Messenger ﷺ and the monumental spiritual outpouring of ethical Islamic principles and Qur'ānic teachings dissolved many a strife. But nonetheless, humankind is predisposed to variation between its ilk, and thus this fated principle of divergence has taken its course among Muslims over their extended history. At this juncture, we are not invested in defining the causes and bases for the divergence that took place after the passing of the Holy Prophet ﷺ (whether it had been morally sanctionable, the result of independent reasoning (*ijtihād*) between the Muslims, collusion, a power struggle, etc.). However, what concerns us here is that the Prophet's departure formed an important milestone in the timeline of Islam. Indeed, rapid was that snowball effect which precipitated a great schism within Islam's adherents, eventually leading to entire schools of thought and movements that would brawl with each other and even shed one another's blood in the name of the self-same creed.

We do not aim to place the responsibility of this rift upon anyone, but rather we aim to usher a dispelling of this state. Although we may disagree in our interpretation of the Qur'ān and Sunnah—disagreeing to the extent that one of us may look at its text and conclude that an action is obligatory while another may not, or one of us may look at a specific verse of the Qur'ān and believe it is a testament to the virtue of a specific historical personality while another may not, this is all but a natural affair. It is not only exclusive to

Islam but is rather seen in the history of all religions because of the human mind's limitations in uncovering truth.

However, the issue has become an ordeal because this natural variation has morphed into an unnatural one, whereby people disregard one another and Muslims distance themselves from each other. Rather, in some cases their blood is even shed owing to the negative viewpoint they carry of their brethren. Hence, the Islamic society is disintegrated, and the condition of Muslims is weakened by their internal strife and discord. Even more unfortunate is that the abundance of argumentation and polemics regarding these sectarian differences coupled with the continued development in these fields has wrought even more discord rather than providing positive intellectual reform! Indeed, there is no worth in these intellectual movements when no positive epistemological or practical reform is facilitated through them.

All of the above requires us to pause together in front of our conscience, our religion, our history, and our humanity to ask: what is our obligation? What can we do to transcend this sectarian hatred whose exponential growth we witness day after day in our current climate? How may we preserve the ummah and the society against the flotsam of sectarian strife and its manifestations? How can we erase this in the spirit of avoiding further degeneration into the abyss of sectarian schism? Every day we witness the mutual shedding of Muslim blood under the auspices of defending religion, creed, sect, and faction—to the extent that their internal conflict is even more heinous, cruel, and violent than their conflict with societies foreign to theirs!

The Shīʿi loyal to Imām ʿAlī ﷺ grapples with the Sunnī loyal to Abū Bakr on issues that even the two personalities themselves never surmised! The Ḥanafī and the Ḥanbalī grapple with the Jaʿfarī to an extent hundreds of time more intense than Imām Jaʿfar al-Ṣādiq ﷺ himself disagreed with Abū Ḥanīfa b. Nuʿmān! At the same time, how may we maintain for each adherent to this religion his own identity, uniqueness, beliefs, and thoughts? How may we combine between a fortified and deep relationship in brotherhood and an authentic preservation of the theological and jurisprudential conclusions and beliefs of our fellow Muslims?

To answer such questions, we require a great deal of discourse, however one of the prerequisites is to become more acquainted with one another via an inquisitive mind: in a way that each of us defines clearly for his compatriot his respective identity so that there is no need for vacillation or doubt. Another step is that everyone among us ought to extent his or her hand to the other in the spirit of meeting on the constructive disagreements we may have while leaving aside those which are not. Let us halt the spilling of blood and the picking at the historical scabs of the ummah. Let us halt the transformation of our present to our past such that we regress; rather, let us progress by reinterpreting our history to form a better present and future. Let us recognize the elements of reconcilability and love therein rather than focusing on the elements of alienation and division or making history a vain goal onto itself.

This book is the precise product of apprehending this enormous responsibility; this suppressed conscientious objection; this monumental crisis in which we live; this intense anxiety that looms on our horizon as a society; and this threat imposing on the very existence of Islam itself. We seek to convey that which God has commanded us towards and to assume some of the responsibility towards the world's Muslims upon our shoulders: to speak the truth in times of crisis.

This humble book is an open memorandum to all the Muslims of the world, whether Shīʿa, Sunnī, Ibāḍi, Ṣūfi, etc. It is a memorandum of love and affection, of brotherhood and amity, of truth and sincerity; a memorandum of laying the facts bare and exposing the truth. It is one of critiquing oneself and others, turning a new page, and defining the school of the Ahl al-Bayt and their followers (the Twelver Shīʿa school). We aim to reveal in it the thoughts, investigations, responsibilities, aspirations, visions, concepts, and inferences that are held by the adherents of this faction.

We will briefly summarize their beliefs, jurisprudence, methodologies, relationship with others, viewpoints, achievements, and historical responsibility.

This is a memorandum to the other—every other—within the sphere of Islam to make clear our conceptions and views and to place ourselves on an authentic trajectory. We live in a historically defining moment in the lifespan of this ummah and we seek to answer the call of the moment with this book: to break the siege of history and embark on a new understanding of religion through which we can join hands and rebuild the majesty of a nation that has long formed an essential link in the history of human civilization.

Speaking for a large segment of the school of the Ahl al-Bayt ﷺ, we announce publicly our open memorandum to the world and our fellow brothers of other Muslim schools of thought: a memorandum which invites toward correspondence, communication, peace, safety, and civilized life; a memorandum that inspires us to grant each other rights, respect, appreciation, and optimism; in order that we may build homelands that are fortified from the interior, not shaken by the windy storms of evil, death, and strife. It is a message that will inspire many but may also upset others here and there; especially as we express our clear viewpoints that may be personally disagreeable, even perhaps to some among the Shīʿa. However, we only seek to contextualize ourselves and our beliefs in the wake of the categorizations of today.

It is a memorandum of love, by God's ﷻ permission: a memorandum for sectarian harmony—for our homeland, our nation, our society, and our civilization; and God ﷻ is over what we say a witness!

Ḥaydar Muḥammad Kāmil Ḥubbullāh

10th Ramaḍān, 1436 A.H.

July 28, 2015

Translator's Introduction

بسم الله الرحمن الرحيم

والصلاة والسلام على محمد وأهل بيته الطيبين الطاهرين

In the Name of God, the Beneficent, the Merciful

May salutations be upon Muḥammad and his Blessed and Pure Holy Progeny.

It indeed gives me great pleasure to translate this short treatise on Islamic intrafaith harmony written by Shaykh Ḥaydar Ḥubbullāh, one of the eminent scholars within the Ḥawza seminary of Qum. In the current environment in which we live, strife with sectarian conflict and polemics, Shaykh Ḥaydar's work presents an incisive analysis into the key issues that have impeded the unification of Muslims for centuries and presents concrete and practical solutions to overcome these challenges. Given that Shaykh Ḥaydar has remained a relatively less known figure in the English-speaking world, it would behoove us to introduce a brief biographical sketch of this personality to acquaint the reader with his background. After this, I would like to make some remarks about the English translation that lies before you. Finally, I would like to extend my acknowledgements and gratitude to those who aided this translation endeavor.

Shaykh Ḥaydar Muḥammad Kāmil Ḥubbullāh was born in 1973 in Southern Lebanon to a religious family and completed his primary and intermediate education in his locality. He matriculated into the Ḥawza seminary in the city of Tyre in 1988 and studied the introductory and intermediary levels of seminary training with several reputable scholars. In 1995, he immigrated to the Islamic Republic of Iran to complete his higher-level seminary studies; in doing so, he attended the advanced fiqhī and usūlī discussions among many highly reputable āyatullāhs and marājiʿ (sources of emulation), including the likes of Sayyid Maḥmūd Hāshimī ash-Shāhrūdī ﷺ, Āyatullāh Jawādī Āmulī, Āyatullāh Bāqir al-Īrawānī, Āyatullāh Ḥusayn Waḥīd Khurāsānī, and Sayyid Kamāl al-Ḥaydarī. He subsequently received dual master's degrees in reputable Iranian universities in the fields of both Qur'ānic/Ḥadīth sciences and Islamic fiqh and usūl al-fiqh. Recognizing the need to expand his expertise beyond solely the Islamic sciences, he went on further to obtain a doctorate in Comparative Religion and Christian Theology. He remains a very active academic figure as the chief editor of two ongoing journals: *al-Nuṣūṣ al-Muʿāṣirah* (Contemporary Texts) and *al-Ijtihād wa al-Tajdīd* (Religious Interpretation and Reform). In addition to writing several authoritative works in fiqh, ḥadīth, and usūl, Shaykh Ḥaydar has supervised several doctoral dissertations in Iranian universities; he is also a strong advocate of intrafaith studies as he is actively involved in projects to codify all authentic Prophetic ḥadīth across all sects and to consolidate all Imāmi hadith on jurisprudence into a single corpus. Among his excellent works in the vein of sectarian unity is the volume before you, which has thus far already been translated into Persian and Urdu.

Translation is always a delicate art and requires carefully wording the author's imports while preserving an idiomatic flow to the text; we hope that our translation will meet this prerequisite for the reader. Throughout the text, we have endeavored to include our own footnotes when deemed necessary for further understanding or for reference to relevant source material that may benefit the reader. Wherever possible, we have strived to make sure these are resources that are in English and freely available online, predominantly through the site www.al-Islam.org. We have also attempted to include Arabic terms in parentheses or italics where deemed necessary and have utilized a standard Hans-Wehr transliteration for Arabic terms. We have not italicized proper names given that these are not technically Islamic terms. Of course, should there be any shortcomings in translation, we accept full responsibility for these limitations and would highly appreciate any feedback from the readers.

Finally, I would like to extend my acknowledgements for this humble work. I dedicate this translation endeavor to our Twelfth Imām عجل الله تعالى فرجه الشريف, who would most certainly expect us to be united as an ummah. I would also like to thank my dear wife Fatemah for being very supportive and understanding as

I often spent several hours at a time busy at this translation. I would also like to thank my mother Latifa for her insightful comments in discussion about this work. Next, I would like to thank Sayyid Ali Imran for his vital support through the project in editing the text of this translation and for his gracing this text with a foreword of his own; in fact, his translation of the section on the Ṣaḥābah was adapted into this translation work. Finally, I would like to acknowledge and thank you—dear reader—for your role in advance in reading and hopefully implementing this text in your life to bridge the gaps in our Muslim community. "And my success is only through God; upon Him I rely and towards Him I turn."

Dr. M.H. Jaffer

14th Rajab al-Murajjab, 1443 A.H.

February 16, 2022

Foreword

﴿وَٱعْتَصِمُوا۟ بِحَبْلِ ٱللَّهِ جَمِيعًا وَلَا تَفَرَّقُوا۟ ۚ وَٱذْكُرُوا۟ نِعْمَتَ ٱللَّهِ عَلَيْكُمْ إِذْ
كُنتُمْ أَعْدَآءً فَأَلَّفَ بَيْنَ قُلُوبِكُمْ فَأَصْبَحْتُم بِنِعْمَتِهِۦٓ إِخْوَٰنًا وَكُنتُمْ عَلَىٰ شَفَا
حُفْرَةٍ مِّنَ ٱلنَّارِ فَأَنقَذَكُم مِّنْهَا ۗ كَذَٰلِكَ يُبَيِّنُ ٱللَّهُ لَكُمْ ءَايَٰتِهِۦ لَعَلَّكُمْ
تَهْتَدُونَ﴾

﴾wa-ʿtaṣimū bi-ḥabli llāhi jamīʿan wa-lā tafarraqū wa-dhkurū niʿmata llāhi ʿalaykum ʾidh kuntum ʾaʿdāʾan fa-ʾallafa bayna qulūbikum fa-ʾaṣbaḥtum bi-niʿmatihī ʾikhwānan wa-kuntum ʿalā shafā ḥufratin mina n-nāri fa-ʾanqadhakum minhā ka-dhālika yubayyinu llāhu lakum ʾāyātihī laʿallakum tahtadūn [a]﴿

﴾Hold fast, all together, to God's cord, and do not be divided [into sects]. And remember God's blessing upon you when you were enemies, then He brought your hearts together, so you became brothers with His blessing. And you were on the brink of a pit of Fire, whereat He saved you from it. Thus does God clarify His signs for you so that you may be guided.﴿[2]

I first came across the name of Shaykh Ḥaydar Ḥubullah in 2012, when I happened to read one of his articles translated in English. The overwhelmingly exhaustive research, distilled coherence, depth of discussion, and the presentation of arguments were quite striking to me. I had not been fortunate enough to come across such lucid and developed ideas until

---

2 Sūrat Āl ʿImrān, Verse 103.

then. I did not know who this Shaykh was but eventually came to know he was one – of thousands - of teachers in the seminary of Qom.

On May 5th, 2016, as a matter of happenstance, a colleague of mine from Kuwait hosted a private gathering at his house in Qom, inviting the Shaykh as a guest. I was still unfamiliar with the works of the Shaykh and had only recalled the article I had read few years earlier. As we began to discuss different topics in that gathering, I was astonished to see his grasp on various subjects. Still, my initial recollections from that gathering did not spike my interest in his works entirely, as I had come across many scholars in the seminary with a formidable grasp of their subjects of interest.

That gathering however, did result in some further readings of his works, with his novel ideas and rejuvenating approaches becoming much clearer for me. Two books that had an immediate impact on my time in the seminary were his Naẓarīyyah al-Sunnah and Ḥujjīyyah al-Sunnah. The former is a work of intellectual history, analyzing the phenomenon of solitary reports and how different trends and groups throughout Shīʿī history dealt with this phenomenon, while the latter is an extensive work addressing pertinent issues of theology and legal theory pertaining to the Sunnah. These were exactly the discussions I had aspired to be acquainted with when I came to the seminary; discussions that are perhaps difficult and challenging, ignored and only implicitly addressed.

As opportunities arose, I eventually began to regularly attend Shaykh Ḥaydar's classes and benefited immensely from his precision, ideas, and humble persona during my time in Qom.

Shaykh Ḥaydar is one of the few gems who has rigorously and critically engaged with not just the Islamic and Western intellectual traditions, but philosophical schools from both, along with having exhaustively engaged with the Abrahamic textual tradition. He remains somewhat of an anomaly, in being able to bring together the rich Islamic textual tradition with the ever expanding intellectual sciences.

Shaykh Ḥaydar's grasp on both areas allows him to offer an entirely novel framework of thinking about religious discourse, combining discussions from philosophy of religion, legal theory, Qur'ānic and Ḥadīth sciences, providing reasonable practical solutions to live a religious and spiritual life in the modern era.

This is precisely what he has managed to do in his Memorandum on Intrafaith Harmony. Sloganeering around intrafaith unity climaxed in the 20th century, even finding noticeable support in segments of the higher echelons of Muslim seminaries, yet sectarian violence and propaganda has arguably only worsened in the 21st century. As Shīʿa-Sunnī relationships worsened in the Muslim world, particularly in Iraq, Yemen, Afghanistan, Syria and Pakistan, some prominent students of knowledge from Oman approached Shaykh Ḥaydar asking him to write a treatise addressing and clarifying various points of contentions between the two schools of thought.

Topics such as justice and cursing of the companions, intercession, certain jurisprudential positions, corruption of the Qur'ān, and other similar topics that often make up the bulk of polemical discussions and sectarianism. Unfortunately, exhaustive, and critical engagement with these subjects is rarely seen by either sect, with neither willing to critically reflect on their own positions and stances. Eventually, these discussions make their way onto various media platforms in very desacralized forms - to only further fuel discord. In this context, calling for unity without addressing and clarifying these concepts for the masses is tantamount to carrying water in a sieve.

In line with what Āyatullāh Muḥammad Ḥusayn Kāshif al-Ghiṭā' ؒ (d. 1373/1953) had done in *Aṣl al-Shīʿa wa Uṣūluhā* or Shaykh Muḥammad Riḍā Muẓaffar ؒ (d. 1964) in his *ʿAqā'id al-Imāmīyyah*, Shaykh Ḥaydar chose to write a book outlining the beliefs of the Shīʿa, but also offer brief socio-cultural observations on some matters. The difference between the two aforementioned works and the Shaykh's

Memorandum is that the latter also offers critical observations on some of the stances taken by the Shīʿa themselves and gives them food for thought.

One of the most fascinating sections of the book is the Shaykh's discussion on the Companions of the Prophet ﷺ. Given the highly sensitive nature of the topic, the balanced approach he has taken to deal with the subject is to be applauded. Laying down the premise of granting the right of ijtihād in historical matters and reinforcing the notion that incorrect ijtihād does not constitute disbelief, he clarifies the Shīʿī position on the companions. While not shying away from the honest truth that Shīʿī jurists have generally considered it permissible to curse some companions who are highly revered by the Ahl al-Sunnah, the Shaykh also brings to light the extent of cursing that was pioneered by the Umayyads, in particular, that of Imām ʿAlī ؑ. The solution, as he articulates it, may lie in a call to self-reflection. Sunnī scholars should strive to uncover a shrouded history, in reassessing the tragedies that befell some companions of the Prophet ﷺ on showing mere loyalty to Imām ʿAlī ؑ, while the Shīʿa should take into consideration several reports from the Imāms ؑ of the Ahl al-Bayt ؑ in which companions of the Prophet ﷺ are highly praised.

In essence, these critical observations open a pathway to work towards a society of Muslims where Shīʿa, Sunnī and as well as other sects, can live with one another with mutual respect and understanding of one another, while not feeling any moral or religious obligation to provoke and incite one another on the basis of their faith.

The common Shīʿī and Sunnī understanding of unity and coexistence is one based on expediency, particularly political expediency, and not a genuine unity that can be arrived at by revisiting certain cultural practices and being more nuanced with some of the theological positions. Unity based on political expedience is often witnessed in the annual Unity Conference that has been held in Tehran since 1987. After being given the privilege to attend this conference three times, I found that the topics of discussions were far more concerned with the politics of the Middle East. While those matters are not of any less significance, there is simply no discussion that I witnessed addressing the crux of many sectarian issues, which are often theological in nature.

The Shaykh believes there are a significant number of Muslim scholars, either Sunnī or Shīʿa who theologically and practically believe in a genuine form of unity and coexistence amongst the Muslims. This work in essence is a brief expression of the stance of such scholars. The book however does not suffice with simply explaining points of contention, rather the Shaykh concludes his work with several practical solutions.

This is a unique work written at a level comprehensible for the laity and it will surely open the mind of the reader willing to look at things from a different perspective.

Sayyid Ali Imran

10th Shawwal, 1443 A.H.

May 11th, 2022

What is the Value of this Nature of Memoranda?

As we begin this discussion with the dear reader, it is natural for a question to arise within our minds: what is the purpose of this type of memoranda? What will we obtain from writing such words? Will anyone listen to this call? Will it be actualized, or will this content itself be leveraged for polemical interests? These questions are certainly legitimate, and I will not hide the fact—dear reader—that I have thought about them long and hard in deep concern about this topic. At the start of this memorandum, we would therefore like to clarify a few key points:

Our Memorandum: Between the Voice of the Conscience and a Responsible Reality

Before anything, we face the responsibilities that are laid upon our shoulders by religion, moral values, and our conscience to not stay quiet about what is occurring and to participate in changing the current situation—to speak the truth even if against ourselves, our parents, and our relatives as the Noble Qur'ān itself has stated.

This memorandum therefore has inherent value in my humble opinion—specifically in absolving us from responsibility in front of God ﷻ, history, and humankind. It indicates that we attempted to do what was within our capacity, although still yet speech is a low form of faith.[3] However, we must not relinquish all of faith just because we are not able to offer it at its most complete level; rather we present at least the lowest form of it so that we may experience a sense of psychological peace, bearing in mind that "God does not burden any soul beyond its capacity."[4]

Once we depart from this personal station of "conscience," we shall perceive that we are between two choices: either we submit ourselves to the current dilemma or we come forward to offer the trifle that we can muster to improve it. When each of us considers being faced with these two options, I believe it is only natural that we would pursue endeavoring and striving to improve it, as mere surrender to the current clime will produce nothing but the eventual demise of this great ummah.

---

[3] This is a reference to the famous Prophetic hadith narrated by both Shīʿa and Sunnī sources as follows:

من رأى منكم منكراً فليغيره بيده، فان لم يستطع فبلسانه، فان لم يستطع فبقلبه، وذلك أضعف الإيمان

"Whoever among you sees evil then let him change it with his own hand; and if he cannot do so, then by his tongue; if he cannot do so, then by his heart—although this is the weakest form of faith."

ʿAbd al-Razzāq, *al-Muṣannaf*, Vol. 3, p. 275.

[4] Sūrat al-Baqarah, Verse 286.

Everything is Possible, Hence Let us Practice Our Roles in Our Own Domains of Influence

What we have outlined as our recommendations in this memorandum very well may not be actualized, however it is possible for each of us to play his or her respective role in his domain of influence. Therefore, let us try to at least endeavor towards this, for if we do not succeed at the larger level then it suffices us to be proud in the fact that we have aided to some degree in preventing the deterioration of the ummah—even at the level of a teacher in a university or religious institution, a religious scholar, a media correspondent, a writer, a mother, a father, etc. We all have our own ability to effect change, however minor; when these efforts are accumulated, then at the very best we achieve a productive outcome and at the very least we hamper further deterioration. As the aphorism goes, when drops of small water are accumulated, they can form a stream. The logic of action and change dictates that we should participate even in the smallest manner, as without such grassroot efforts the development of a current is not possible. Indeed, if each of us thought about the triviality of the single drops of water we offer, nothing would be finalized, and a spirit of change and reform would never materialize.

The Noble Qur'ān and the Language of Aspiring for the Future

This is also the same logic that we find in the Qur'ān: a constant optimism because hope inherently has a constructive effect whereas despair leaves us with no strength or conscientiousness.

As God ﷻ has stated:

﴿أَلَمْ نَشْرَحْ لَكَ صَدْرَكَ﴾

'a-lam nashraḥ laka ṣadrak [a]

﴿وَوَضَعْنَا عَنْكَ وِزْرَكَ﴾

wa-waḍaʿnā ʿanka wizrak [a]

﴿الَّذِي أَنْقَضَ ظَهْرَكَ﴾

lladhī 'anqaḍa ẓahrak [a]

﴿وَرَفَعْنَا لَكَ ذِكْرَكَ﴾

wa-rafaʿnā laka dhikrak [a]

﴿فَإِنَّ مَعَ الْعُسْرِ يُسْرًا﴾

fa-ʾinna maʿa l-ʿusri yusra n

﴿إِنَّ مَعَ الْعُسْرِ يُسْرًا﴾

ʾinna maʿa l-ʿusri yusra n

﴿*Did We not open* your *breast for* you *and relieve* you *of your burden which [almost] broke* your *back? Did We not exalt* your *name? Indeed ease accompanies hardship. Indeed ease accompanies hardship.*﴾[5]

God ﷻ also states:

﴿فَلَمَّا فَصَلَ طَالُوتُ بِٱلْجُنُودِ قَالَ إِنَّ ٱللَّهَ مُبْتَلِيكُم بِنَهَرٍ فَمَن شَرِبَ مِنْهُ فَلَيْسَ مِنِّى وَمَن لَّمْ يَطْعَمْهُ فَإِنَّهُۥ مِنِّىٓ إِلَّا مَنِ ٱغْتَرَفَ غُرْفَةًۢ بِيَدِهِۦ فَشَرِبُوا۟ مِنْهُ إِلَّا قَلِيلًا مِّنْهُمْ فَلَمَّا جَاوَزَهُۥ هُوَ وَٱلَّذِينَ ءَامَنُوا۟ مَعَهُۥ قَالُوا۟ لَا طَاقَةَ لَنَا ٱلْيَوْمَ بِجَالُوتَ وَجُنُودِهِۦ قَالَ ٱلَّذِينَ يَظُنُّونَ أَنَّهُم مُّلَٰقُوا۟ ٱللَّهِ كَم مِّن فِئَةٍ قَلِيلَةٍ غَلَبَتْ فِئَةً كَثِيرَةًۢ بِإِذْنِ ٱللَّهِ وَٱللَّهُ مَعَ ٱلصَّٰبِرِينَ﴾

[5] Sūrat al-Sharḥ, Verses 1-6.

﴾fa-lammā faṣala ṭālūtu bi-l-junūdi qāla ʾinna llāha mubtalīkum bi-naharin fa-man shariba minhu fa-laysa minnī wa-man lam yaṭʿamhu fa-ʾinnahū minnī ʾillā mani ghtarafa ghurfatan bi-yadihī fa-sharibū minhu ʾillā qalīlan minhum fa-lammā jāwazahū huwa wa-lladhīna ʾāmanū maʿahū qālū lā ṭāqata lanā l-yawma bi-jālūta wa-junūdihī qāla lladhīna yaẓunnūna ʾannahum mulāqū llāhi kam min fiʾatin qalīlatin ghalabat fiʾatan kathīratan bi-ʾidhni llāhi wa-llāhu maʿa ṣ-ṣābirīn [a]﴿

﴾As Saul set out with the troops, he said, 'God will test you with a stream: anyone who drinks from it will not belong to me, but those who do not drink from it will belong to me, barring someone who draws a scoop with his hand.' But they drank from it, [all] except a few of them. So when he crossed it along with the faithful who were with him, they said, 'We have no strength today against Goliath and his troops.' Those who were certain they will encounter God said, 'How many a small party has overcome a larger party by God's will! And God is with the patient.'﴿[6]

And God ﷻ states:

﴿الَّذِينَ قَالَ لَهُمُ النَّاسُ إِنَّ النَّاسَ قَدْ جَمَعُوا لَكُمْ فَاخْشَوْهُمْ
فَزَادَهُمْ إِيمَانًا وَقَالُوا حَسْبُنَا اللَّهُ وَنِعْمَ الْوَكِيلُ﴾

---

[6] Sūrat al-Baqarah, Verse 249.

﴿*a lladhīna qāla lahumu n-nāsu 'inna n-nāsa qad jamaʿū lakum fa-khshawhum fa-zādahum 'īmānan wa-qālū ḥasbunā llāhu wa-niʿma l-wakīl u*﴾

﴿فَانْقَلَبُوا بِنِعْمَةٍ مِنَ اللَّهِ وَفَضْلٍ لَمْ يَمْسَسْهُمْ سُوءٌ
وَاتَّبَعُوا رِضْوَانَ اللَّهِ ۗ وَاللَّهُ ذُو فَضْلٍ عَظِيمٍ﴾

﴿*fa-nqalabū bi-niʿmatin mina llāhi wa-faḍlin lam yamsashum sū'un wa-ttabaʿū riḍwāna llāhi wa-llāhu dhū faḍlin ʿaẓīm in*﴾

﴿إِنَّمَا ذَٰلِكُمُ الشَّيْطَانُ يُخَوِّفُ أَوْلِيَاءَهُ فَلَا
تَخَافُوهُمْ وَخَافُونِ إِنْ كُنْتُمْ مُؤْمِنِينَ﴾

﴿*'innamā dhālikumu sh-shayṭānu yukhawwifu 'awliyā'ahū fa-lā takhāfūhum wa-khāfūni 'in kuntum mu'minīn a*﴾

﴿*Those to whom the people said, 'All the people have gathered against you; so fear them.' That only increased them in faith, and they said, 'God is sufficient for us, and He is an excellent trustee.' So they returned with God's blessing and grace, untouched by any evil. They pursued the pleasure of God, and God is dispenser of a great grace.*

That is only Satan frightening his followers! So fear them not, and fear Me, should you be faithful.﴿[7]

This memorandum—as we pointed out in our introduction—does not only represent the Shīʿas, the Sunnīs, or other factions. Even though it has been written by a single author, it represents the persuasion of a vast scope of the Muslim world's sociological groups including scholars, aristocrats, teachers, thinkers, researchers, activists, reporters, writers, etc. It is an expression of what a large segment of the ummah believes, but yet may not express due to marginalization. Nonetheless, the spirit of religion, ethics, and humanism summons their presence in this tome.

In this work we do not speak on behalf of a specific sect, country, political party, or political movement; we also do not claim that what we have written represents the view of the Shīʿa authorities (*al-marjiʿiyyah*) or all their subgroups. We do not maintain that it represents the view of the fiqhī institutions of Ahl al-Sunnah. However, we do believe that it represents the view of a vast number of luminaries among those imbued with knowledge, action, repute, and social standing in this ummah and particularly the Imāmī sect. They make clear their opinion and conviction about what ought to be done and they join hands with other sects—especially those among them who are cultured and are

[7] Sūrat Āl ʿImrān, Verses 173-175.

endowed with a social responsibility—to share with them in these endeavors regarding what is required in this difficult historical moment. Otherwise, we do not claim to embody the view of a specific sect or group—we speak on behalf of ourselves and believe that we represent a vast swathe of Muslims and those among the Imāmī sect as well.

Our Message is to Free Religion From Sectarian Excuses for Our Conflicts

This memorandum by no means will solve all issues and we shall never expect that—it is a treatise for circulation in order that we may respond to the relevant issues in an optimal manner; in order that we may think about how to establish definitive algorithms to resolve to the quarrelsome issues. As such, we hope that we may erect a simple landmark in the vast intellectual ocean of work about Islamic harmony.

This memorandum does not suppose that it will solve the impending political issues in Muslim countries, as this is the responsibility and duty of politicians. This memorandum only seeks to shed light on the religious, ethical, and intellectual dimension of the relationship between sects and to present its perspective regarding it while maintaining full recognition that this is not a unidimensional problem. We do not claim that the problems facing the Muslims today are solely of a sectarian nature or that the concerns existing between Shīʿas and Sunnīs that we discussed earlier are the only cause of crisis among Muslims. However, our contention—and we urge your attention—is that the political powers in Muslim countries take advantage of sectarian issues and sects to fuel their political motives. Our duty is therefore to dry out and dispose of this fuel source so that it is not used by those who hurt Muslims, either knowingly or unknowingly.

This subject is therefore of the highest religious value, since any conflict that is based on sectarian tension has the capacity to damage the reputation and stance of religion in the world; in turn, this would strengthen atheistic and areligious movements to grow further and engulf more Muslim youth towards lack of religious and purpose. Indeed, stamping out the religious dimension from our conflicts today is of the highest exigency and serves an important interest for religion in the contemporary world. This is also a message we endorse and a goal towards which we aspire.

Welcoming Constructive Critique and Alternative Viewpoints

We welcome any critical or intellectually honest observations regarding this memorandum from both inside and outside. We hope that it may find sincere voices in our midst and establish an example through leaving a positive, even if minor, impact upon the current stark reality upon which further endeavors may be launched. We hope that reasonable and enlightened voices from other sects among Muslims will listen to this memorandum and come forth to express their concerns, bold criticism, and constructive observations about themselves and others. It is hoped that in the shade of this mutual cooperation, we may reach a deeper, more insightful, and mature perspective, God-willing.

In conclusion, this is our hope, conviction, and approach; it is our outlook for a better future and our religious creed by which we pledge ourselves onto God ﷻ. Indeed, God ﷻ is a witness over our speech, and is the enabler of success and succor. We ask God ﷻ to make our humble effort acceptable and pleasing to Him, and to grant us the success of sincerity of intention, soundness of heart, and purity of spirit.

We ask Him ﷻ to place this in our record of good deeds in the Hereafter,

﴿يَوْمَ لَا يَنْفَعُ مَالٌ وَلَا بَنُونَ﴾

﴾yawma lā yanfaʿu mālun wa-lā banūn [a]﴿

﴿إِلَّا مَنْ أَتَى اللَّهَ بِقَلْبٍ سَلِيمٍ﴾

﴿'illā man 'atā llāha bi-qalbin salīm in﴾

﴿the day when neither wealth nor children will avail, except him who comes to God with a sound heart﴾*[8]

﴿آمَنَ الرَّسُولُ بِمَا أُنْزِلَ إِلَيْهِ مِنْ رَبِّهِ وَالْمُؤْمِنُونَ ۚ كُلٌّ آمَنَ بِاللَّهِ وَمَلَائِكَتِهِ وَكُتُبِهِ وَرُسُلِهِ لَا نُفَرِّقُ بَيْنَ أَحَدٍ مِنْ رُسُلِهِ ۚ وَقَالُوا سَمِعْنَا وَأَطَعْنَا ۖ غُفْرَانَكَ رَبَّنَا وَإِلَيْكَ الْمَصِيرُ﴾

﴿'āmana r-rasūlu bi-mā 'unzila 'ilayhi min rabbihī wa-l-mu'minūna kullun 'āmana bi-llāhi wa-malā'ikatihī wa-kutubihī wa-rusulihī lā nufarriqu bayna 'aḥadin min rusulihī wa-qālū sami'nā wa-'aṭa'nā ghufrānaka rabbanā wa-'ilayka l-maṣīr u﴾

﴿The Apostle has faith in what has been sent down to him from his Lord, and all the faithful. Each [of them] has faith in God, His angels, His scriptures and His apostles.

[8] Sūrat al-Shu'arā', Verses 88-89.

* That is, a heart that is free from the love of the world.

[They declare,] 'We make no distinction between any of His apostles.' And they say, 'We hear and obey. Our Lord, forgive us, and toward You is the return.'﴿[9]

[9] Sūrat al-Baqarah, Verses 285-286.

The Shīʿa and their Religious Beliefs: A Synopsis of the Imāmī Sect

Introduction

The Imāmī Twelver school of thought adheres to a large number of the same core tenets shared by other Muslims; the areas of difference that it has with other sects are also highly disputed within those other sects themselves. That is to say: the points of theological divergence between the Imāmīs and other Muslim sects are the self-same contentious areas that are found between those Islamic sects such as the Māturīdīs, the Salafīs, the Ashʿarīs, the Muʿtazilīs, the Ṣūfīs, the Ibāḍīs, the Zaydīs, etc. We see the same applies to the differences found in issues of Islamic history (*tārīkh*) and jurisprudence (*fiqh*). Our role here is to attempt to present a highly abridged overview of the theological and jurisprudential precepts of the Imāmīs as an introduction to delving into our core discussion.

The Precepts of Belief in the Imāmi Sect

The Twelver Imāmī sect believes in the general Islamic and religious tenets with a set of unique beliefs that set it apart and bears witness to their unique independent reasoning (*ijtihād*) in matters of Islamic creed based on their traditional and rational understanding of Qur'ān and Sunnah. The following is a brief synopsis regarding their beliefs in reference to Divine Unity (*tawḥīd*),

God's ﷻ justice (*'adl*), fate and destiny (*qaḍā'* and *qadr*), God's ﷻ attributes (*al-ṣifāt*), prophethood (*nubuwwah*), divine viceregency (*imāmah*), and the Hereafter (*ma'ād*). We will discuss these on the following axes:

The First Axis: Divinity (*al-ulūhīyyah*)[10]

The Imāmī sect believes in the existence of God ﷻ and that He is not dependent in His existence upon anything. They also believe in His Essential Unity (*waḥdānīyyah*): that He is one, single, unique, self-sufficient, not taking any spouse or child, that He has no partner in His Dominion, and that He created everything and apportioned it precisely.[11] In the Imāmī sect, God ﷻ is the First, the Last, the Apparent, the Hidden and is Omniscient. He is God ﷻ in the Heavens and the Earth.[12]

---

[10] Among the excellent references to understand Shī'ite theology is the work of Āyatullāh Murtaḍā Muṭahharī in his article entitled "*An Introduction to 'Ilm al-Kalām*" translated by Alī Qulī Qarā'ī.

[11] Sūrat al-Furqān, Verse 2.

[12] Sūrat al-Ḥadīd, Verse 3 and Sūrat al-An'ām, Verse 3. The author is attempting to show that the Shī'a Imāmī faction derives its beliefs about God ﷻ from the Qur'ān as does any other Muslim sect. This is specifically done to establish common ground with other Muslims while at the same time dispelling misconceptions that Shī'a believe in an alternative Qur'ān.

As it states in the Qurʾān:

﴿هُوَ اللَّهُ الَّذِي لَا إِلَٰهَ إِلَّا هُوَ ۖ عَالِمُ الْغَيْبِ
وَالشَّهَادَةِ ۖ هُوَ الرَّحْمَٰنُ الرَّحِيمُ﴾

﴾huwa llāhu lladhī lā ʾilāha ʾillā huwa ʿālimu l-ghaybi wa-sh-shahādati huwa r-raḥmānu r-raḥīm[u]﴿

﴿هُوَ اللَّهُ الَّذِي لَا إِلَٰهَ إِلَّا هُوَ الْمَلِكُ الْقُدُّوسُ السَّلَامُ الْمُؤْمِنُ الْمُهَيْمِنُ
الْعَزِيزُ الْجَبَّارُ الْمُتَكَبِّرُ ۚ سُبْحَانَ اللَّهِ عَمَّا يُشْرِكُونَ﴾

﴾huwa llāhu lladhī lā ʾilāha ʾillā huwa l-maliku l-quddūsu s-salāmu l-muʾminu l-muhayminu l-ʿazīzu l-jabbāru l-mutakabbiru subḥāna llāhi ʿammā yushrikūn[a]﴿

﴿هُوَ اللَّهُ الْخَالِقُ الْبَارِئُ الْمُصَوِّرُ ۖ لَهُ الْأَسْمَاءُ الْحُسْنَىٰ ۚ يُسَبِّحُ لَهُ مَا
فِي السَّمَاوَاتِ وَالْأَرْضِ ۖ وَهُوَ الْعَزِيزُ الْحَكِيمُ﴾

﴾huwa llāhu l-khāliqu l-bāriʾu l-muṣawwiru lahu l-ʾasmāʾu l-ḥusnā yusabbiḥu lahū mā fī s-samāwāti wa-l-ʾarḍi wa-huwa l-ʿazīzu l-ḥakīm[u]﴿

﴾He is God—there is no god except Him—Knower of the sensible and the Unseen, He is the Beneficent, the Merciful. He is God—there is no god except Him—the Sovereign, the All-holy, the All-benign, the Securer, the All-conserver, the All-mighty, the All-compeller, the All-magnanimous. Clear is God of any partners that they may ascribe [to Him]! He is God, the Creator, the Maker, the Former. To Him belong the Best Names. Whatever there is in the heavens glorifies Him and [whatever there is in] the earth, and He is the All-mighty, the All-wise.[13]﴿*

Therefore, for the Imāmī sect, God ﷻ has the Most Beautiful Names and the Most Exalted Attributes. He exists without any contingency, exalted above all matter or substance, form or corporeality, and image or likeness. He has no dimensions and is not subject to time, space, condition, quantity, location, or temporality. He is not an accident (*ʿarḍ*) that would require a substance (mawḍuʿ), an effect (maʿlūl) that would require a cause (*ʿillah*), nor a contingent entity (*mumkin*) that would require a Necessary Existent (*wājib al-wujūd*). He is not defective in any manner such that he would require another that is perfect. He is not dependent on any other, rather everything is dependent on Him. He is not seeable, touchable, or

[13] Sūrat al-Ḥashr, Verse 22-24.

* Or 'the Impeccable.'

sensible with any of the five senses. Nothing resembles Him and He has no rival or competitor.

Rather He is as the Qurʾān states:

﴿فَاطِرُ السَّمَاوَاتِ وَالْأَرْضِ ۚ جَعَلَ لَكُمْ مِنْ أَنْفُسِكُمْ أَزْوَاجًا وَمِنَ الْأَنْعَامِ أَزْوَاجًا ۖ يَذْرَؤُكُمْ فِيهِ ۚ لَيْسَ كَمِثْلِهِ شَيْءٌ ۖ وَهُوَ السَّمِيعُ الْبَصِيرُ﴾

﴿fāṭiru s-samāwāti wa-l-ʾarḍi jaʿala lakum min ʾanfusikum ʾazwājan wa-mina l-ʾanʿāmi ʾazwājan yadhraʾukum fīhi laysa ka-mithlihī shayʾun wa-huwa s-samīʿu l-baṣīr u﴾

﴿لَهُ مَقَالِيدُ السَّمَاوَاتِ وَالْأَرْضِ ۖ يَبْسُطُ الرِّزْقَ لِمَنْ يَشَاءُ وَيَقْدِرُ ۚ إِنَّهُ بِكُلِّ شَيْءٍ عَلِيمٌ﴾

﴿lahū maqālīdu s-samāwāti wa-l-ʾarḍi yabsuṭu r-rizqa li-man yashāʾu wa-yaqdiru ʾinnahū bi-kulli shayʾin ʿalīm un﴾

﴿The originator of the heavens and the earth, He made for you mates from your own selves, and mates of the cattle, by which means He multiplies you. Nothing is like Him, and He is the All-hearing, the All-seeing. To Him belong the keys of the heavens and the earth:*

He expands the provision for whomever He wishes, and tightens it [for whomever He wishes]. Indeed He has knowledge of all things. ﴿[14]

The theology of the Imāmī sect pertaining to God ﷻ revolves around some important concepts, the most prominent being the following:

a. Divine Unity (*al-Tawḥīd*)[15]

After the substantiation of the Divine Holy Essence, the Imāmī Shīʿa believe in tawḥīd, which is the basis of Islam and they consider this as carrying several imports and manifestations:

1. Unity of Essence (*Al-Tawḥīd al-Dhātī*)

This implies that God ﷻ is One with no likeness (*mathīl*), counterpart (*naẓīr*), rival (*ʿadīl*), or similarity (*shabīh*). Furthermore, it implies that His Essence is simple without absolutely any parts or

[14] Sūrat al-Shūrā, Verses 11-12.

* In case the *kāf* in *ka-mithlihī* is not taken as redundant, the meaning will be, 'There is nothing like His likeness.'

[15] A beautiful exposition of the significance of tawḥīd within Shīʿa Islām may be found in the book "At-Tawhid or Monotheism" by the late Āyatullāh Muḥammad Taqī Miṣbāh Yazdī ؒ translated into English by N. Tawheedi.

compartmentalization within it. Therefore, any trinitarian precept imposing this type of differentiation is invalid. Some of the Imāmī scholars differentiate between these two forms of unity by calling negation of particularization "The Unity of Singleness" (*Al-Tawḥīd al-Aḥadī*) and the negation of a counterpart "The Unity of Oneness" (*al-Tawḥīd al-Wāhidī*).

2. Unity of Attributes (*Al-Tawḥīd al-Ṣifātī*)

The Imāmī sect holds that God ﷻ has all attributes of perfection, encompassing the Masculine Majestic (*jalālīyyah*) and Feminine Beautiful (*jamālīyyah*) attributes; these include omniscience (*al-ʿilm*), omnipotence (*al-qudrah*), eternal life (*al-ḥayāt*), absolute providence (*al-irādah*), hearing (*al-samʿ*), seeing (*al-baṣar*), creatorship (*al-khalq*), perpetuity (*al-qidam*), impenetrability (*al-ṣamadīyyah*), self-sufficiency (*al-ghinā*), etc. His Essential Attributes (*al-ṣifāt al-dhātīyya*h) are not external to His Essence, but rather are themselves subsumed in it. Their multiplicity is only a product of our mortal inability to fathom Him ﷻ. But God Himself ﷻ has no compartmentalization such that a part of Him could be called "power," "knowledge," etc. Instead, His knowledge is self-same with his power in a single Essence.

Meanwhile, His Active Attributes (*al-ṣifāt al-fiʿlīyyah*)—such as creating and sustaining—are qualities derived from the station of His action. When He creates, He is given the title "Creator." As a result, the Imāmī sect has divided God's ﷻ attributes into Essential and Active—the former being part and parcel unified in God's Essence while the latter being accidental, only ascribed to Him because of His actions.

3. Unity of the Creatorship (*Al-Tawḥīd al-Khāliqī*)

This implies that there is no Creator except God ﷻ, and every other designer is himself designed; rather God ﷻ is as He describes himself in the Qur'ān:

﴿فَتَبَارَكَ اللَّهُ أَحْسَنُ الْخَالِقِينَ﴾

﴿*fa-tabāraka llāhu ʾaḥsanu l-khāliqīn*﴾

﴿*So blessed is God, the best of creators!*﴾[16]

It is He who created everything but is Himself neither created nor originating from something else. There is a consensus among the Imāmī sect and rather among nearly all theologians that this world is created and contingent. However, some of the philosophers have

---

[16] Sūrat al-Mu'minūn, Verse 14.

proposed that the created world is also eternal, stating that just because this is the case does not imply that it is self-sufficient or that it does not require the Necessary Existent (*wājib al-wujūd*). They state that God ﷻ is still its Creator, but that it is perpetual in time (*qadīm zamānī*), essentially contingent (*ḥādith dhātī*), and ontologically wanting (*faqīr wujūdī*) for its existence upon God ﷻ. They therefore believe that the pinnacle of Divine perfection is embodied in the fact that the Divine Effulgence (*al-fayḍ al-ilāhī*) is unceasing and continues to create and sustain without beginning or end.

4. Unity of Lordship (*Al-Tawḥīd al-Rubūbī*)

They intend by this that the manager of this world is the self-same One who created it. He did not delegate it to another and consign Himself to the periphery, such that He should have no active role in His creation. Rather, to Him belongs the absolute management (*al-tadbīr al-muṭlaq*).

It is therefore as God Himself ﷻ has said in His book:

﴿إِنَّ رَبَّكُمُ اللَّهُ الَّذِي خَلَقَ السَّمَاوَاتِ وَالْأَرْضَ فِي سِتَّةِ أَيَّامٍ ثُمَّ اسْتَوَىٰ
عَلَى الْعَرْشِ ۖ يُدَبِّرُ الْأَمْرَ ۖ مَا مِنْ شَفِيعٍ إِلَّا مِنْ بَعْدِ إِذْنِهِ ۚ ذَٰلِكُمُ اللَّهُ
رَبُّكُمْ فَاعْبُدُوهُ ۚ أَفَلَا تَذَكَّرُونَ﴾

﴿'inna rabbakumu llāhu lladhī khalaqa s-samāwāti wa-l-'arḍa fī sittati 'ayyāmin thumma stawā ʿalā l-ʿarshi yudabbiru l-'amra mā min shafīʿin 'illā min baʿdi 'idhnihī dhālikumu llāhu rabbukum fa-ʿbudūhu 'a-fa-lā tadhakkarūn ᵃ﴾

﴿Indeed your Lord is God, who created the heavens and the earth in six days, and then settled on the Throne, directing the command. There is no intercessor, except by His leave. That is God, your Lord! So worship Him. Will you not then take admonition?﴾*[17]

And He has further stated:

﴿قُلْ مَنْ يَرْزُقُكُمْ مِنَ السَّمَاءِ وَالْأَرْضِ أَمَّنْ يَمْلِكُ السَّمْعَ وَالْأَبْصَارَ وَمَنْ يُخْرِجُ الْحَيَّ مِنَ الْمَيِّتِ وَيُخْرِجُ الْمَيِّتَ مِنَ الْحَيِّ وَمَنْ يُدَبِّرُ الْأَمْرَ ۚ فَسَيَقُولُونَ اللَّهُ ۚ فَقُلْ أَفَلَا تَتَّقُونَ﴾

﴿qul man yarzuqukum mina s-samā'i wa-l-'arḍi 'am-man yamliku s-samʿa wa-l-'abṣāra wa-man yukhriju l-ḥayya mina l-mayyiti wa-yukhriju l-mayyita mina l-ḥayyi wa-man yudabbiru l-'amra fa-sa-yaqūlūna llāhu fa-qul 'a-fa-lā tattaqūn ᵃ﴾

[17] Sūrat Yūnus, Verse 3.

* Confer 13:2 and 32:5.

﴿فَذَٰلِكُمُ اللَّهُ رَبُّكُمُ الْحَقُّ ۖ فَمَاذَا بَعْدَ الْحَقِّ إِلَّا الضَّلَالُ ۖ فَأَنَّىٰ تُصْرَفُونَ﴾

﴿*fa-dhālikumu llāhu rabbukumu l-ḥaqqu fa-mādhā baʿda l-ḥaqqi ʾillā ḍ-ḍalālu fa-ʾannā tuṣrafūn* [a]﴾

﴿Say, *'Who provides for you out of the sky and the earth? Who controls [your] hearing and sight, and who brings forth the living from the dead and brings forth the dead from the living, and who directs the command?' They will say, 'God.'* Say, *'Will you not then be wary [of Him]?' That, then, is God, your true Lord. So what is there after the truth except error? Then where are you being led away?*﴾[18]

We will soon touch upon the belief of some in the Imāmī sect in the Existential Guardianship (*al-Wilāyah al-Takwīnīyyah*) of the Ahl al-Bayt ﷺ when we treat the subject of Imāmah as well as when we talk about the mutual intrafaith issues with other schools of thought.

5. Unity of Worship (*Al-Tawḥīd al-ʿIbādī*) and the Prohibition Against Prostrating to Other than God ﷻ

Among the Shīʿa, this implies that it is categorically prohibited to worship anyone except God ﷻ. Furthermore, it is contended that exclusive worship of a

[18] Sūrat Yūnus, Verse 31-32.

single God ﷻ is the cornerstone and slogan of all the Prophets ﷺ. We are the servants of God ﷻ alone and the slogan of Islam is what God ﷻ has stated:

﴿إِيَّاكَ نَعْبُدُ وَإِيَّاكَ نَسْتَعِينُ﴾

﴿*'iyyāka na'budu wa-'iyyāka nasta'īn u*﴾

﴿*You [alone] do we worship, and to You [alone] do we turn for help.*﴾[19]

As such, the Shī'a do not pray, fast, make pilgrimage, or pay alms-tax except with the intention of achieving proximity to God ﷻ. They see these actions as religiously invalid and obligatory to repeat—rather they are strictly prohibited—if they should be done for any other than God ﷻ. Hence, we find in their books a clear prohibition of prostrating with the intention of worship to any other than God ﷻ.

The late Sayyid Abul-Qāsim al-Khū'ī ﵀ (d. 1413 A.H.), one of the greatest sources of emulation (*marja'*) in the Shī'a Imāmī world, has stated: "It is prohibited to prostrate to any other entity other than God ﷻ, regardless of whether it is infallible or not. Therefore, that which the Shī'a do at the mausoleums of the Imāms ﷺ must be solely for God ﷻ in expressing gratitude in

[19] Sūrat al-Fātiḥah, Verse 5.

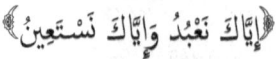

granting them the opportunity to visit them (peace be upon them) and be present at their mausoleums.[20]

6. What about the fact that the Shīʿa Imāmis give their children names like "The Servant of Ḥusayn (ʿAbdul-Ḥusayn)," etc. ?

As for the fact that the Imāmi sect names their children such names as Servant of Ḥusayn, of Zahrā, of Muḥsin, of ʿAlī, of Mahdī, etc. then it should be known that this is becoming relatively less popular now and that it is not intended to signify slavehood (*ʿubūdiyyah*) to them in the sense of worship, but rather with the meaning of subservience (*al-khidmah*). It is to signify that we are the servants of the Prophet ﷺ and his family ﵈ and that we obey them and follow their instructions. This all goes without saying that ʿAbdul Ḥusayn is a common name used even in the African Sunnī world.

Furthermore, there is no sacred text from the hadith of the Ahl al-Bayt ﵈ that mentions such epithets or encourages their use. This phenomenon in fact did not exist in the lifespan of Shīʿīsm until the last couple centuries. The best witness to the fact that the Shīʿa books of biography, historical accounts, encyclopedias,

[20] Khūʾī, Āyatullāh Sayyid Abū al-Qāsim Mūsawī, *Minhāj al-Ṣāliḥīn*, Vol. 1, p. 179, q. 659.

and hadith personalities (*'ilm al-rijāl*) do not mention any such names among the Imāmī sect.

Even if we were to surmise that there is a problem from an Islamic legal standpoint, as some Sunnī scholars have judged, it remains a jurisprudential difference; it has no relevance to Shīʻa ʻaqīdah and does not indicate worship of created beings as this would annul the tenet of tawḥīd. How could this be when the Shīʻa Imāmī sect itself makes it clear that such epithets imply servitude and do not carry any polytheistic import? We will deal with this issue further—God willing—when we discuss the Shīʻa Imāmī rituals, their relationship with the Ahl al-Bayt 🕊, their visits to their purified graves, and what may be perceived as polytheism within these rites.

b. The Divine Names and Attributes (*al-Asmāʾ wa al-Ṣifāt al-Ilāhiyyah*)

Within the Imāmī sect, the Divine Names are broken into Positive and Negative Attributes:

The Positive Confirmatory Attributes (*al-Ṣifāt al-Thubūtiyyah*)

This implies that every perfection belongs to God ﷻ and the division is further split into Essential Attributes and Active Attributes:

i. Essential Attributes (*al-Sifāt al-Dhātiyyah*)

This refers to those attributes that are inseparable from the Divine Essence, including:

1. The First Attribute: Omniscience (*al-ʿilm*)

God ﷻ is Omniscient—innately, in perpetuity, and absolutely—of all things past, present, and future. There is no limit to the Divine Knowledge and it subsumes all generalities and specificities. However, some of the Muslim philosophers—Shīʿa and Sunnī—have a particular theory about God's ﷻ knowledge of specificities. Nonetheless, the majority of Muslim theologians have defined the Divine Knowledge as timeless, absolute, and encompassing everything without limits. They rely on both rational (*ʿaqlī*) and traditional (*naqlī*) sources to substantiate this viewpoint, including the verses of the Qur'ān such as:

﴿وَعِنْدَهُ مَفَاتِحُ الْغَيْبِ لَا يَعْلَمُهَا إِلَّا هُوَ ۚ وَيَعْلَمُ مَا فِي الْبَرِّ وَالْبَحْرِ ۚ وَمَا تَسْقُطُ مِنْ وَرَقَةٍ إِلَّا يَعْلَمُهَا وَلَا حَبَّةٍ فِي ظُلُمَاتِ الْأَرْضِ وَلَا رَطْبٍ وَلَا يَابِسٍ إِلَّا فِي كِتَابٍ مُبِينٍ﴾

﴾*wa-ʿindahū mafātiḥu l-ghaybi lā yaʿlamuhā ʾillā huwa wa-yaʿlamu mā fī l-barri wa-l-baḥri wa-mā tasquṭu min waraqatin ʾillā yaʿlamuhā wa-lā ḥabbatin fī ẓulumāti l-ʾarḍi wa-lā raṭbin wa-lā yābisin ʾillā fī kitābin mubīn in*﴿

﴾*With Him are the treasures of the Unseen**; *no one knows them except Him. He knows whatever there is in land and sea. No leaf falls without His knowing it, nor is there a grain in the darkness of the earth, nor anything fresh or withered but it is in a manifest Book.*﴿[21]

Another verse which implies the same is as follows:

﴿وَقَالَ الَّذِينَ كَفَرُوا لَا تَأْتِينَا السَّاعَةُ ۖ قُلْ بَلَىٰ وَرَبِّي لَتَأْتِيَنَّكُمْ عَالِمِ الْغَيْبِ ۖ لَا يَعْزُبُ عَنْهُ مِثْقَالُ ذَرَّةٍ فِي السَّمَاوَاتِ وَلَا فِي الْأَرْضِ وَلَا أَصْغَرُ مِنْ ذَٰلِكَ وَلَا أَكْبَرُ إِلَّا فِي كِتَابٍ مُبِينٍ﴾

﴾*wa-qāla lladhīna kafarū lā taʾtīnā s-sāʿatu qul balā wa-rabbī la-taʾtiyannakum ʿālimi l-ghaybi lā yaʿzubu ʿanhu mithqālu dharratin fī s-samāwāti wa-lā fī l-ʾarḍi wa-lā ʾaṣgharu min dhālika wa-lā ʾakbaru ʾillā fī kitābin mubīn in*﴿

---

[21] Sūrat al-Anʿām, Verse 59.

* Or 'the keys of the Unseen.'

﴾*"The faithless say, 'The Hour will not overtake us.'* Say, *'Yes indeed, by my Lord, it will surely come to you.'—The Knower of the Unseen, not [even] an atom's weight escapes Him in the heavens or in the earth, nor [is there] anything smaller than that nor bigger, but it is in a manifest Book,*﴿[22]

Divine Knowledge and the Question of Badāʾ

There are certainly folks who imagine that the Imāmī belief in the doctrine of manifestation (*al-badāʾ*) would imply the attribution of ignorance to God ﷻ or that something is made apparent to Him after it had been abstruse. However, the reality is that this belief, as explained clearly by the Imāmī theologians, does not imply other than the Absolute Power (*al-qudrah*) of God ﷻ in changing His decisions in accordance with His pre-existing knowledge. Thus, for instance, He changes the lifespan of an individual due to his supplication; this could never be the result of ignorance, may God ﷻ give us refuge, but rather it is a mere modification in the Divine Tablet (*al-lawḥ*) of affirmation/negation. This is done in such a way that the foregone and forthcoming decisions are both recorded in the Preserved Tablet (*al-lawḥ al-maḥfūẓ*) and the Tablet of Certain Destiny (*lawḥ al-qaḍāʾ al-ḥatmī*).

---

[22] Sūrat Saba, Verse 3.

Therefore, the doctrine of manifestation only means that God ﷻ manifests to us something that we witness and imagine a change has taken place; however, this change had already been recorded in the Tablet of Certain Destiny with God ﷻ. In other words, the doctrine of manifestation is only the set of rules for existential change. Therefore, for instance, if an individual maintains family ties (*ṣilat al-raḥm*), his lifespan increases from fifty to sixty years. The rules of change existing in the physical world, also known as cause-and-effect, is the alternative terminology for the doctrine of manifestation. Although all the while, the changes that preceded and are forthcoming in the plane of existence have already been recorded with God ﷻ in his Preserved Tablet.

Although the Arabic word al-badā' may be controversial for some it has also been narrated in some of the books of Ahl al-Sunnah.[23] There are additionally several uses of this concept in Sunnī ḥadīth regarding the influence

[23] Please see *Saḥīḥ al-Bukhārī*, Vol. 4, p. 146 where Abū Hurayrah is narrated to have said on the authority of the Prophet ﷺ, "بدا لله في الأقرع والأبرص" which some commentators interpret to mean the self-same principle of badā' among the Shī'a Imāmīs.

of ṣadaqah and duʿāʾ in changing destiny.[24] The problem is surely not in the term itself, because the concept is the vital concern upon which we ought to base our understanding of the Imāmī faction; not based on the word or the form of expression used.

The Imāmī faction interprets the issue of badāʾ as crucial in explaining the influence of our acts of piety in our worldly lives, including providing background for the philosophy of supplication and its justifications, etc.

2. The Second Attribute: Omnipotence (*al-qudrah*)

God ﷻ is Omnipotent to act or not act with full will (*al-mashīʾa*), determination (*al-irādah*), and choice (*al-ikhtiyār*). This faculty is permanent, timeless, and absolutely essential to Him unconditionally. As for those situations which are impossible to actualize, such as combining contradictions, then it should be said that the incapacity is not in the Doer (*al-fāʿil*) and His

---

[24] As an example of this, we see the following hadith narrated in *Sunan al-Tirmidhī*, ḥadīth 2139:

عَنْ سَلْمَانَ قَالَ قَالَ رَسُولُ اللَّهِ صَلَّى اللَّهُ عَلَيْهِ وَسَلَّمَ لَا يَرُدُّ الْقَضَاءَ إِلَّا الدُّعَاءُ وَلَا يَزِيدُ فِي الْعُمْرِ إِلَّا الْبِرُّ

"Nothing repels the divine decree but supplication, and nothing increases longevity but righteousness.""

ability, but rather in the object (*al-maf'ūl bihī*) and its potentiality.[25] Just as the Imāmī theologians have relied upon rational and traditional sources to substantiate God's ﷻ knowledge, they have done the same regarding his omnipotence: for the attribution of incapacity to God ﷻ goes against His Absolute Perfection and makes Him contingent upon others. It is thus that God ﷻ states:

وَأُخْرَىٰ لَمْ تَقْدِرُوا عَلَيْهَا قَدْ أَحَاطَ اللَّهُ بِهَا ۚ
وَكَانَ اللَّهُ عَلَىٰ كُلِّ شَيْءٍ ﴿قَدِيرًا﴾

﴾*wa-'ukhrā lam taqdirū 'alayhā qad 'aḥāṭa llāhu bihā wa-kāna llāhu 'alā kulli shay'in qadīra* [n]﴿

﴾*And other [spoils] which you have not yet captured: God has comprehended them, and God has power over all things.*﴿[26]

3. The Third Attribute: Ever-Livingness (*al-ḥayāt*)

This is among the attributes over which there is contention in its interpretation, with some stating that it is subsumed within His attributes of knowledge,

---

[25] This is a summative answer against those who ask questions such as "Can God make a rock so heavy he cannot lift it?" In other words, this question that is being asked is nonsensical and therefore it is not possible, not due to any weakness in God himself.

[26] Sūrat al-Fatḥ, Verse 21.

power, and determination. In any case, there is no possibility of death or annihilation for His Divine Nature. God ﷻ states this when he describes Himself in the Qurʾān:

﴿اللَّهُ لَا إِلَٰهَ إِلَّا هُوَ الْحَيُّ الْقَيُّومُ ۚ لَا تَأْخُذُهُ سِنَةٌ وَلَا نَوْمٌ ۚ لَهُ مَا فِي السَّمَاوَاتِ وَمَا فِي الْأَرْضِ ۗ مَنْ ذَا الَّذِي يَشْفَعُ عِنْدَهُ إِلَّا بِإِذْنِهِ ۚ يَعْلَمُ مَا بَيْنَ أَيْدِيهِمْ وَمَا خَلْفَهُمْ ۖ وَلَا يُحِيطُونَ بِشَيْءٍ مِنْ عِلْمِهِ إِلَّا بِمَا شَاءَ ۚ وَسِعَ كُرْسِيُّهُ السَّمَاوَاتِ وَالْأَرْضَ ۖ وَلَا يَئُودُهُ حِفْظُهُمَا ۚ وَهُوَ الْعَلِيُّ الْعَظِيمُ﴾

﴾llāhu lā ʾilāha ʾillā huwa l-ḥayyu l-qayyūmu lā taʾkhudhuhū sinatun wa-lā nawmun lahū mā fī s-samāwāti wa-mā fī l-ʾarḍi man dhā lladhī yashfaʿu ʿindahū ʾillā bi-ʾidhnihī yaʿlamu mā bayna ʾaydīhim wa-mā khalfahum wa-lā yuḥīṭūna bi-shayʾin min ʿilmihī ʾillā bi-mā shāʾa wasiʿa kursiyyuhu s-samāwāti wa-l-ʾarḍa wa-lā yaʾūduhū ḥifẓuhumā wa-huwa l-ʿaliyyu l-ʿaẓīm ᵘ﴿

﴾God—there is no god except Him— is the Living One, the All-sustainer. Neither drowsiness befalls Him nor sleep. To Him belongs whatever is in the heavens and whatever is on the earth. Who is it that may intercede with Him except with His permission? He knows that which is before them and that which is behind them, and they do not comprehend anything of His knowledge except what He wishes.

His seat embraces the heavens and the earth, and He is not wearied by their preservation, and He is the All-exalted, the All-supreme.﴿[27]

ii. Active Attributes (*al-Ṣifāt al-Fiʿlīyyah*)

This includes a number of attributes, such as His Creatorship (*al-Khāliqīyyah*), His Sustainership (*al-Rāziqīyyah*), His Executionership (*al-Mudabbirīyyah*), His Lordship (*al-Rubūbīyyah*), His Irresistibility (*al-Qāhirīyyah*), etc. Among these attributes is His being a speaker (*al-Mutakallim*), and it is well-accepted among the Imāmī faction that speech with his creation is orchestrated through revelation (*al-waḥy*), or the sending of a messenger-angel (*al-rasūl*), or from behind a barrier (*al-ḥijāb*), in accordance with God's ﷻ words:

﴿وَمَا كَانَ لِبَشَرٍ أَنْ يُكَلِّمَهُ اللَّهُ إِلَّا وَحْيًا أَوْ مِنْ وَرَاءِ حِجَابٍ أَوْ يُرْسِلَ
رَسُولًا فَيُوحِيَ بِإِذْنِهِ مَا يَشَاءُ ۚ إِنَّهُ عَلِيٌّ حَكِيمٌ﴾

﴾*wa-mā kāna li-basharin ʾan yukallimahu llāhu ʾillā waḥyan ʾaw min warāʾi ḥijābin ʾaw yursila rasūlan fa-yūḥiya bi-ʾidhnihī mā yashāʾu ʾinnahū ʿaliyyun ḥakīm un*﴿

﴾*It is not [possible] for any human that God should speak to him* except through revelation or from behind a curtain,**

[27] Sūrat al-Baqarah, Verse 255.

or send a messenger* who reveals by His permission whatever He wishes. Indeed He is all-exalted, all-wise.[28]

His speech occurs through the creation of voices that the Prophets can hear, and thus it is among the Active Attributes and not the Essential Ones, as it emerges from his Creativeness. It is by the same token that the Imāmī theologians define God's ﷻ speech (*al-kalām*) as His action or the result of His action; God ﷻ has stated:

﴿قُلْ لَوْ كَانَ الْبَحْرُ مِدَادًا لِكَلِمَاتِ رَبِّي لَنَفِدَ الْبَحْرُ قَبْلَ أَنْ تَنْفَدَ كَلِمَاتُ رَبِّي وَلَوْ جِئْنَا بِمِثْلِهِ مَدَدًا﴾

﴿qul law kāna l-baḥru midādan li-kalimāti rabbī la-nafida l-baḥru qabla ʾan tanfada kalimātu rabbī wa-law jiʾnā bi-mithlihī madada ⁿ﴾

---

28 Sūrat al-Shūrā, Verse 55.

* Or 'it does not behoove any human that God should speak to him.'

* As from a tree, as in the case of Mūsā ﵇.

* That is, an angel.

﴾Say, "If the seas were pens for the words of my Lord, the seas would be extinguished before the words of my Lord, even should we doubly append them with their equivalent in likeness.﴿[29]

It is in this context that the Imāmī scholars believe that the Noble Qur'ān is God's ﷻ Created Speech (*al-kalām al-makhlūq*). It is not timeless but rather created, as His speech is an action; this viewpoint goes against many of the scholars of Ahl al-Sunnah.[30]

Additionally, among these attributes is His Wisdom (*al-ḥikmah*), meaning that His actions are done with utmost perfection in a way that every element is in its suitable place, for He is absolutely transcendent from doing anything which is unsuitable.[31]

The Negative Attributes (*al-Ṣifāt al-Salbīyyah*)

These attributes reflect the concept of God's ﷻ transcendence (*al-tanzīh*) in the belief of the Imāmī sect, and they subsume many attributes.

---

[29] Sūrat al-Kahf, Verse 109.

[30] The notable exception to this among Ahl al-Sunnah is the Muʿtazilī theological school of thought, which agrees with the Shīʿa that the Qur'ān is makhlūq.

[31] It is upon this principle that the Shīʿa theologians establish the principle of *lutf*, namely that God's ﷻ designs always facilitate the path towards obedience to Him.

Among these is that God ﷻ is not a physical body and cannot be seen or apprehended with any of the senses—neither in this world nor in the hereafter. He is not physical and is not bound in any time, space, or direction such that he can be seen. However, there is no objection to His detection by the insight of the heart. The Imāmī theologians have relied—in addition to rational arguments—upon the text of the Noble Qurʾān in adopting this viewpoint:

﴿لَا تُدْرِكُهُ الْأَبْصَارُ وَهُوَ يُدْرِكُ الْأَبْصَارَ ۖ وَهُوَ اللَّطِيفُ الْخَبِيرُ﴾

﴾lā tudrikuhu l-ʾabṣāru wa-huwa yudriku l-ʾabṣāra wa-huwa l-laṭīfu l-khabīru﴿

﴾The sights do not apprehend Him, yet He apprehends the sights, and He is the All-attentive, the All-aware.﴿*[32]

Furthermore, he is not limited, separable, nor divisible; he does not possess any such attributes that are characteristic of deficiency. He has no partner, likeness, rival, or comrade; He is not mergeable or capable of being subsumed within another. As for the Qurʾānic verses and hadith which seem to suggest God's ﷻ

---

[32] Sūrat al-Anʿām, Verse 103.

* Or 'All-gracious.' Confer. 22:63; 31:16; 33:34; 67:14.

likeness, perceptibility, or physicality, the Imāmī theologians have interpreted these to exclude their prima facie meanings (*ma'ānīhā al-awwalīyyah*) and have advanced linguistic defenses to this end. They have contributed a great deal in reference to this issue and it behooves those interested in this regard to refer to their long treatises in Qur'ānic exegesis and theology.[33]

iii. Divine Justice (*al-'adl al-ilāhī*)

The Imāmī Shī'a believe in divine justice and therefore do not believe that God ﷻ is the agent of any oppression to any single entity; rather his actions are the pinnacle of justice and equity, as the textual sources indicate and the intellects profess. God ﷻ says:

﴿شَهِدَ اللَّهُ أَنَّهُ لَا إِلَٰهَ إِلَّا هُوَ وَالْمَلَائِكَةُ وَأُولُو الْعِلْمِ قَائِمًا بِالْقِسْطِ ۚ
لَا إِلَٰهَ إِلَّا هُوَ الْعَزِيزُ الْحَكِيمُ﴾

﴿*shahida llāhu 'annahū lā 'ilāha 'illā huwa wa-l-malā'ikatu wa-'ulū l-'ilmi qā'iman bi-l-qisṭi lā 'ilāha 'illā huwa l-'azīzu l-ḥakīm* [u]﴾

---

[33] Many excellent references may be pointed out in this vein, however a great introduction to the Shī'a theological approach can be found in the book "*Discursive Theology*" by Professor Ali Rabbānī Gulpāygānī and translated by Mansoor Limba. Specifically, reference Chapter 18: The Attributes of the Khabariyyah.

﴾*God bears witness that there is no god except Him —and [so do] the angels and those who possess knowledge— maintainer of justice, there is no god but Him, the Almighty, the All-wise.*﴿[34]

Rather, God ﷻ does not command except to justice, therefore how could He not be just?!

As God ﷻ states in His Book:

﴿إِنَّ اللَّهَ يَأْمُرُكُمْ أَنْ تُؤَدُّوا الْأَمَانَاتِ إِلَىٰ أَهْلِهَا وَإِذَا حَكَمْتُمْ بَيْنَ النَّاسِ أَنْ تَحْكُمُوا بِالْعَدْلِ ۚ إِنَّ اللَّهَ نِعِمَّا يَعِظُكُمْ بِهِ ۗ إِنَّ اللَّهَ كَانَ سَمِيعًا بَصِيرًا﴾

﴾*ʾinna llāha yaʾmurukum ʾan tuʾaddū l-ʾamānāti ʾilā ʾahlihā wa-ʾidhā ḥakamtum bayna n-nāsi ʾan taḥkumū bi-l-ʿadli ʾinna llāha niʿimmā yaʿiẓukum bihī ʾinna llāha kāna samīʿan baṣīra n*﴿

﴾*Indeed God commands you to deliver the trusts to their [rightful] owners, and, when you judge between people, to judge with fairness. Excellent indeed is what God advises you. Indeed God is all-hearing, all-seeing.*﴿[35]

---

[34] Sūrat Āl ʿImrān, Verse 18.

[35] Sūrat al-Nisāʾ, Verse 58.

In yet another place, God ﷻ states:

﴿إِنَّ اللَّهَ يَأْمُرُ بِالْعَدْلِ وَالْإِحْسَانِ وَإِيتَاءِ ذِي الْقُرْبَىٰ وَيَنْهَىٰ عَنِ الْفَحْشَاءِ وَالْمُنكَرِ وَالْبَغْيِ ۚ يَعِظُكُمْ لَعَلَّكُمْ تَذَكَّرُونَ﴾

﴿'inna llāha ya'muru bi-l-ʿadli wa-l-'iḥsāni wa-'ītā'i dhī l-qurbā wa-yanhā ʿani l-faḥshā'i wa-l-munkari wa-l-baghyi yaʿiẓukum laʿallakum tadhakkarūn [a]*﴾*

﴾Indeed God enjoins justice and kindness and generosity towards relatives, and He forbids indecency, wrong, and aggression. He advises you, so that you may take admonition.﴿[36]

The primary thrust of this belief—in addition to the Qur'ān and Sunnah—is that the Imāmīs believe in the existence of rational beauty and ugliness (*al-taḥsīn wa al-taqbīḥ al-ʿaqliyayn*) and view rationality as the criterion for asserting the ugliness of oppression and the beauty of justice. In the Imāmī view, God ﷻ does not do what is reprehensible due to the perfection of His Essence. He does not oppress people, lie, or violate promises as His Essence naturally yields only beauty and perfection. His justice subsumes both matters of creation (*al-takwīn*) and legislation (*al-tashrīʿ*).

[36] Sūrat al-Naḥl, Verse 90.

Therefore, all that we witness in this world are but manifestations of His Justice; as for what is apparently evil, it must carry underlying benefits for creation even if it might appear as evil at first glance. Even further, there is a philosophical viewpoint adopted by some of the Imāmīs that considers evil as devoid of existence; rather, it is nothingness itself. They have extensive philosophical investigations on this account.[37]

By the same token, God's ﷻ legislation (*sharīʿah*) is imbued with justice and is not at all oppressive; the same applies to His reward and chastisement. He is ultimately Just—rather He is Merciful.

Destiny and Fate (*al-Qaḍāʾ wa al-Qadr*)

The Imāmīs believe in divine decision and decree, but at the same time they believe in the free agency and volition of humankind. Therefore, as the popular adage goes from the Imāms of the Prophetic family عليهم السلام: "There is no predestination (*al-jabr*) and no absolute

[37] For a great exposition of the Shīʿa position on the problem of evil, please see the excellent essay entitled "*Divine Justice and the Problem of Evil*," by Shaykh Ghulam Husayn Adeel.

relegation (*al-tafwīḍ*), rather the affair is between the two."[38]

Therefore, Divine foreknowledge regarding volitional action does not obligate predestination; to the contrary, it obligates free-will in their view. God's ﷻ knowledge that so-and-so will perform a particular act of disobedience volitionally necessitates that the act is performed by free-will and not by force; otherwise, there would be a deficiency in the knowledge of God. ﷻ That is, God's ﷻ knowledge is that one will perform an action based on his/her own free will and if it was done instead out of force, this would not be in correspondence with God's ﷻ knowledge.[39]

The Second Axis: Prophethood (*al-Nubūwwah*) and Messengership (*al-Risālah*)

Just as other sects of Muslims, the Imāmīs believe in the principle of divine appointment (*al-biʿthah*) and prophethood, viewing it as a manifestation of The Divine Effulgence and Providence upon humankind.

---

[38] This ḥadīth can be found on the authority of Imām Jaʿfar al-Ṣādiq ؑ in the Shīʿa ḥadīth collection by Majlisī, ʿAllamah Muḥammad Bāqir, *Biḥār al-Anwār*, Vol. 5, p. 17, ḥadīth number 28.

[39] This is a summative refutation of the common fallacy that stipulates that God's ﷻ foreknowledge of our actions necessitates predestination. A more detailed refutation can be found in the work of Murtaḍā Muṭahharī entitled "*Man and His Destiny.*"

They see the rational mind as being incapable of comprehending all existential benefits and harms (*al-maṣālih wa al-mafāsid*) and often subject to the evil inclinations of the lower soul (*al-nafs al-ammārah*): therefore, the appointment of prophets and messengers in order to guide humankind to the truth and the correct path was mandatory.[40]

The objective of prophethood is establishment of the belief in Divine Unity and worship of The Only One True God ﷻ: the belief in Divine Unity should flow into every aspect of human life and there should be recognition of Him as the only Agent of Existence, such that one should be infused with pleasure, submission, acceptance, accession, humility, and worship to Him ﷻ. In a similar vein, another objective of prophethood is the establishment of justice and equity as well as the abolition of schisms between people in order that they may all hold fast together to God's ﷻ rope of succor. In the establishment of prophethood is the completion of evidence (*itmām al-ḥujjah*) upon God's ﷻ servants in order that God ﷻ may have the most binding evidence

[40] When it is remarked by Shīʿa scholars that it was mandatory upon God ﷻ to send Prophets, this does not imply an external force necessitating this duty upon God ﷻ. Rather, it stems from God's ﷻ own essential attributes of justice and wisdom that he would not leave his creation without adequate guidance.

against the people while they may have no counterevidence against Him. As God ﷻ has said:

﴿لَقَدْ أَرْسَلْنَا رُسُلَنَا بِالْبَيِّنَاتِ وَأَنْزَلْنَا مَعَهُمُ الْكِتَابَ وَالْمِيزَانَ لِيَقُومَ النَّاسُ بِالْقِسْطِ﴾

﴿la-qad ʾarsalnā rusulanā bi-l-bayyināti wa-ʾanzalnā maʿahumu l-kitāba wa-l-mīzāna li-yaqūma n-nāsu bi-l-qisṭi﴾

﴿Certainly We sent Our apostles with manifest proofs, and We sent down with them the Book and the Balance, so that mankind may maintain justice﴾[41]

Therefore, the sending of Prophets is a binding exigency derived from Divine Providence, Generosity, and Favor. This is how the Imāmīs recognize the Prophets and such is their belief about them. They believe in all the Prophets and it has been narrated in some of their traditions that the total number of Prophets approximates 124,000; in establishing the large number of Prophets in the course of history, they rely on the Qurʾānic verse:

[41] Sūrat al-Ḥadīd, Verse 25.

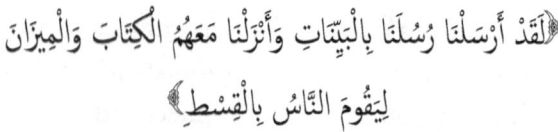

﴿إِنَّا أَرْسَلْنَاكَ بِالْحَقِّ بَشِيرًا وَنَذِيرًا ۚ وَإِن مِّنْ أُمَّةٍ إِلَّا خَلَا فِيهَا نَذِيرٌ﴾

﴾*'innā 'arsalnāka bi-l-ḥaqqi bashīran wa-nadhīran wa-'in min 'ummatin 'illā khalā fīhā nadhīr*un﴿

﴾*Indeed We have sent* you *with the truth as a bearer of good news and as a warner; and there is not a nation but a warner has passed in it.*﴿[42]

In the view of the Imāmīs, prophethood is recognized either by:

1) A clear and decisive attestation from a previous Prophet established by indubitability (*al-naṣṣ al-qaṭʿī*) or

2) Eyewitness accounts, circumstantial evidence, or proofs on the basis of certainty that establish his appointment (*al-adillah al-yaqīnīyyah*).

In reference to the latter, the chief of all of these is coming forth with something that is impossible for anyone else to replicate (a miracle or *muʿjizah*). This would establish that he has been furnished with Divine Succor; otherwise, it would follow that God ﷻ has misguided his servants by allowing the execution of a

[42] Sūrat Fāṭir, Verse 24.

miracle at the hand of a non-Prophet. Given that such a thing is reprehensible, and God ﷻ is beyond all defects and ugliness, it follows that this cannot take place. When prophethood is thus established, it becomes incumbent to follow, obey, have faith, and believe in the aforesaid prophet.

The Imāmīs—as the rest of Muslims—understand prophethood as being a Divinely-appointed station not amenable to attainment by mortal means. The esoteric connection of a Prophet with the metaphysical is wrought either through seeing, hearing, or otherwise communicating with an angel; hence, prophethood is not at all wrought by creative innovation and neither are the prophets simply social reformers as advocated by some contemporary thinkers.[43] Rather it is an elevated station beyond even the most exceptional of human achievements.

a. Infallibility (*al-ʿiṣmah*) of the Prophets and Messengers ﻊ

Since a Prophet is not a regular individual, the majority of the Imāmīs have adopted the view of categorical infallibility: in receiving revelation, in delivering it, both before and after his appointment, before and after adolescence (*al-bulūgh*), and in secret and in private.

[43] As an example of modern-day scholars who advocate for such ideas, please see the writings of Abdolkarīm Soroush.

This infallibility applies to every sin or act of disobedience whether large or small and to every mistake in propagating religion—rather it pertains even to every possible deterrent that would lead to people foregoing his claim to prophethood, such as nobility of lineage, etc.[44]

However, there is a dispute among the Imāmis in reference to two issues:

1. Heedlessness of the Prophet ﷺ (*sahw al-nabī*): wherein the majority have ruled that heedlessness is not tenable, while Shaykh Ṣadūq ؒ (d. 381 A.H.) as well as his teacher Ibn al-Walīd ؒ among others accepted the possibility of heedlessness on the basis of traditions and hadiths that have authentic chains or are even considered successive (*mutawātir*).[45]

---

[44] For more details on this issue, please reference the work of Sayyid Muḥammad Rizvī entitled *"The Infallibility of the Prophets in the Qurʾān."*

[45] Mutawātir is a term used in the ḥadīth sciences to describe a report that is narrated by so many individuals that the likelihood of it being fabricated or not having occurred is extremely small. There are different types of mutawātir, the two major categorizations being described as lafẓī (a ḥadīth that is narrated almost word-for-word by several individuals) and maʿnawī (a ḥadīth whose general import is shared across many narrators). A full discussion of mutawātir is beyond the scope of this text and is often covered in advanced seminary studies.

2. Mistakes in external affairs (*al-khaṭā' fī al-mawḍū'āt al-khārijiyyah*): in other words, is it possible for the Prophet ﷺ to make an error in issues that do not pertain to religion, such as missing a target in archery, etc.? Many have claimed that this is not possible, while others have allowed for it and said it does not affect his prophethood or reputation.

b. The Belief in the Muḥammadan Message

Aforementioned is the general framework that the Imāmīs have outlined for prophethood and they have applied it as well to the Muḥammadan prophethood in particular, accepting the prophethood and messengership of Muḥammad b. 'Abdillah b. 'Abd al-Muṭṭalib and accepting his miracle as the Noble Qur'ān. Meanwhile they differ in the nature and extent of other non-Qur'ānic miracles, among which they mention the splitting of the moon (*shaqq al-qamar*), the night journey to al-Aqṣa and the heavenly ascent (*al-Isrā' wa al-Mi'rāj*), etc. although there are some specific disputes in reference to these.

c. The Universal and Eternality of the Muḥammadan Message

The Muḥammadan message is distinguished among the Imāmīs—as it is for other Muslims—as universal, eternal, and complete. It is by the same token the finality of Divine messages, abrogating all previous religious paths. Therefore, anyone who claims prophethood after the Prophet Muḥammad ﷺ is deviant from the path of truth—either a falsifier or delirious. Additionally, the Muḥammadan message is also distinguished by the belief that its carrier—Muḥammad ﷺ—is the most perfect of humans, the choicest of them, and the seal and jewel of the Prophets عليهم السلام. There is no creation who is more honorable, perfected, or elevated in station with God ﷻ; it is obligatory upon humankind to obey him, love him, perpetuate his remembrance, revere his station in their memories, and respect and appreciate him. Nonetheless, despite his elevated rank, Muḥammad ﷺ is not a god, creator, or sustainer of the world—rather he is a creation as the rest of God's ﷻ creations.

d. The Sources of the Qur'ān and Sunnah: The Question of Distortion (*al-taḥrīf*)

As the Qur'ān is the constitution of this Muḥammadan message, the Shīʿa believe in it in its fullest. The most prominent scholars and the majority of the Imāmīs believe the Qur'ān is free from any distortion—either additions or omissions—and they hold that what is in our hands today is the book of God ﷻ as it was sent down to His Holy Prophet Muḥammad ﷺ.

Meanwhile a very small minority of scholars have held the possibility of distortion only in the sense of omission, such as Shaykh Ḥusayn al-Nūrī ؒ (d. 1320 AH); this group has based their view on some narrations that are present in both Shīʿa and Sunnī ḥadīth sources and it has been the subject of much controversy, as those who are familiar with the Imāmī works on the Qurʾānic sciences, theology, and tafsīr may already know.

As for distortion in the true imports of the Qurʾān (*al-taḥrīf al-maʿnawī*) in the sense of misguided exegesis, then this is seen as possible and present. The same goes for the variant readings of the Qurʾān (*al-qirāʾāt*), which some Imāmīs have accepted as decisive and others have considered to be solitary reports (*akhbār al-āḥād*).

In addition to the Qurʾān as an epistemological source for religion, the Shīʿa have also accepted the noble Prophetic tradition, as the Holy Messenger ﷺ "does not speak out of desire but it is rather revelation sent down."[46] Hence, they accept the Prophetic narrations when they are authenticated, however they did not limit the hadith to only the narrations that stem from the Prophetic household. We will explain this point in the following discussions.

[46] Sūrat al-Najm, Verses 3-4.

The Third Axis: Imāmate (*al-Imāmah*) and Caliphate (*al-Khilāfah*)[47]

The demise of the Holy Prophet ﷺ was a major emotional turning point in the history of Muslims as starting from that time—as the Imāmīs view it—there was a schism in the Muslim nation that continued to fester until it reached its climax in the gruesome massacre that was carried out against the Ahl al-Bayt عليهم السلام in Karbalāʾ. It is entirely possible that the sect of the Shīʿa or the identification Shīʿī did not exist as a separate denomination at that time, however the Imāmīs consider the disputed issues that led to this differentiation alive and well even during that period and most prominent among these was the crisis of caliphate.

a. How do the Shīʿa understand leadership (al-Imāmah) and how do the Sunnīs understand it?

The Imāmī reading of caliphate and leadership differs from the popular reading of the Sunnīs in that the Sunnīs view these issues as mostly historical and jurisprudential; in other words, there is no theological implication to these precepts among the Ahl al-Sunnah.

---

47 Among the excellent English references about Imāmah is the work entitled "*Imāmate and Leadership*" by the late Sayyid Mujtaba Musavi Lari رحمه الله, translated by Dr. Hamid Algar.

As for the Imāmī Shīʿa, they view the issue in a completely different light as they consider it a core principle of theology that every Muslim is bound to believe in: for one who dies while not recognizing the leader of his time عجل الله تعالى فرجه الشريف (*imām zamānihī*) has died the death of ignorance.[48]

The Imāmīs are split in regard to their view of those who reject Imāmah as a theological precept: there are those who view them as disbelievers; then there is the opinion adopted by the majority of latter scholars that they are outwardly Muslim and we treat them with the same relationship that we treat other Shīʿa in the sense of inheritance, marriage, family bonds, and Islamic rights. We do not have any right to call them disbelievers as long as they do not adopt a position of hatred for the Ahl al-Bayt عليهم السلام or establish their religion on the basis of hate for ʿAlī and his offspring—in this latter case, one is considered a hostile (*al-nāṣibī*) and is deemed a disbeliever and a heretic.

---

48 This snippet of the text is derived from a ḥadīth accepted in both Shīʿa and Sunnī major ḥadīth collections. As an example, we will consider the wording of the narration in the *Musnad* of Ibn Ḥanbal Vol. 28, p. 88-89 as follows:

من مات بغير إمام مات ميتة جاهلية

"Whoever dies without an Imām dies a death of ignorance."

b. The Necessity of Imāmate and its Purpose in Shīʿa Belief

Among the Imāmīs, divine leadership (*al-Imāmah*) is considered an inescapable necessity that the religion of Islam requires to propagate the message of the Muḥammadan prophethood and to protect and safeguard it. However, this is not done in the sense of appointment of further prophets, as Prophet Muḥammad ﷺ is no doubt the Final Seal and there can never be another prophet after him. Therefore, God ﷻ ordained that the protection of the Islamic message after the Prophet's ﷺ demise through divine appointment of leaders (*al-a'immah*)—this was done with the goal of allowing the Islamic creed to take on its most pristine form while preserving it from every aberration, fabrication, or distortion whether accidental or deliberate.

The goal of divine leadership is not at all correction of a defect that the Prophet ﷺ had perpetrated (may we seek God's ﷻ refuge)—for he no doubt delivered the message in the best possible form. Rather the goal is to bring forth the best and most correct interpretation of the Qur'ān and Prophetic tradition in accordance with the most perfect transmission; to manage the issues of the Muslims with the most excellent religious administration; to preserve religion with its beliefs, precepts, and divinely-prescribed duties; to confront innovations, aberrations, and fabrications; to defend Muslims and protect their integrity; to establish justice, equity, religious law, and truth in society; to safeguard their unity, integration, honor, and strength; in addition to other duties that the Divinely appointed leader carries after the demise of the Prophet.

c. Imāmate and the Question of Divine Appointment (*al-ta'yīn al-ilāhī*)

The Imāmī belief is that the specific responsibility after the Prophetic period is one of divine designation of a leader and caliph by God ﷻ Himself: nominally, particularly, and by name all at once. It is not accepted that the Muslims be left to choose on their own, and this is established based on many Prophetic traditions that either directly state or implicate the name of Imām 'Alī b. Abī Ṭālib ؑ followed by his children ؑ as the Divinely appointed caliphs to govern the religious and mundane affairs of the Muslims.

This is established on the bases of the following narrations:

a. The hadith of the Prophet's kinsfolk (*ḥadīth al-Dār*) in which the Prophet ﷺ tells Imām 'Alī ؑ: "You are my brother, my inheritor, my vizier, my heir, and my successor after me."[49]

[49] *al-Sīrah al-Ḥalabiyyah*, Vol. 1, p. 460-461.

b. The hadith of the station (*ḥadīth al-Manzilah*), in which the Prophet ﷺ says to him, "Are you not satisfied being unto me like the station of Aaron unto Moses?"[50]

c. The hadith of the pond (*ḥadīth al-Ghadīr*), in which the Messenger ﷺ states, "Oh my Lord, whosoever's master (*mawlā*) I am, then ʿAlī is his master. Oh my Lord, befriend he who befriends him and despise he who despises him."[51]

d. The hadith of the two weighty things (*ḥadīth al-Thaqalayn*) in which he said, "I am leaving amongst you two weighty things, the first of which is heavier than the other: the book of God which is an extension between the Earth and the Heavens, and my offspring the Ahl al-Bayt; for they will never separate until they issue back to me on the Day of Judgement."[52]

e. The hadith of the ship (*ḥadīth al-Safīnah*) in which he says: "My similitude and the similitude of my Ahl al-Bayt is like the Ark of

---

[50] *Ṣaḥīḥ al-Bukhārī*, Vol. 4, p. 208.

[51] *Musnad Aḥmad*, Vol. 1, p. 118.

[52] *Musnad Aḥmad*, Vol. 3, p. 14.

Noah; whoever boards it is saved and whoever tarries behind drowns."[53]

f. The hadith of the protection of the ummah (*ḥadīth Amān al-Ummah*): "The stars have been assigned as protection for the people of the heavens while my Ahl al-Bayt are the protection for my nation."[54]

g. The hadith of the twelve after the Prophet ﷺ (*ḥadīth Ithnay 'Ashar Ba'da al-Nabī*): "There will be after me twelve caliphs, all from Quraish."[55]

As well as many other traditions the majority of which are narrated in both Shī'a and Sunnī books of ḥadīth with chains so numerous that they reach—in some particular cases—the level of successive narrations (*mutawātir*).

---

[53] *Tārīkh al-Baghdād*, Vol. 12, p. 90.

[54] al-Ṭabarānī, Sulaymān, *al-Mu'jam al-Kabīr*, Vol. 7, p. 22.

al-Haythamī, 'Alī, *Majma' al-Zawā'id*, Vol. 9, p. 174.

[55] *Musnad Aḥmad*, Vol. 5, p. 92.

al-Tirmidhī, Muḥammad, *Sunan al-Tirmidhī*, Vol. 3, p. 340.

On the basis of the aforementioned, the Imāmīs view obedience of God ﷻ and his Messenger ﷺ as demanding obedience to their appointed leader for caliphate—there is no option to pick and choose when it comes to God's ﷻ obedience. These clear textual attestations are also coupled to Qur'ānic verses that the ḥadīth support as endorsing the claim of the Ahl al-Bayt ﷺ, such as:

1. The Verse of Mastership (*āyah al-Wilāyah*):

﴿إِنَّمَا وَلِيُّكُمُ اللَّهُ وَرَسُولُهُ وَالَّذِينَ آمَنُوا الَّذِينَ يُقِيمُونَ الصَّلَاةَ وَيُؤْتُونَ الزَّكَاةَ وَهُمْ رَاكِعُونَ﴾

﴿ʾinnamā waliyyukumu llāhu wa-rasūluhū wa-lladhīna ʾāmanū lladhīna yuqīmūna ṣ-ṣalāta wa-yuʾtūna z-zakāta wa-hum rākiʿūn [a]﴾

﴿Your guardian is only God, His Apostle, and the faithful who maintain the prayer and give the zakāt *while bowing down.*﴾[56]

[56] Sūrat al-Māʾidah, Verse 55.

2. The Verse of Purification (*āyah al-Taṭhīr*):

﴿إِنَّمَا يُرِيدُ اللَّهُ لِيُذْهِبَ عَنكُمُ الرِّجْسَ أَهْلَ الْبَيْتِ وَيُطَهِّرَكُمْ تَطْهِيرًا﴾

﴿*ʾinnamā yurīdu llāhu li-yudhhiba ʿankumu r-rijsa ʾahla l-bayti wa-yuṭahhirakum taṭhīra* ⁿ﴾

﴿*Indeed God desires to repel all impurity from you, O People of the Household, and purify you with a thorough purification.*﴾[57]

3. The Verse of Mutual Love (*āyah al-Mawaddah*):

﴿ذَٰلِكَ الَّذِي يُبَشِّرُ اللَّهُ عِبَادَهُ الَّذِينَ آمَنُوا وَعَمِلُوا الصَّالِحَاتِ ۗ قُل لَّا أَسْأَلُكُمْ عَلَيْهِ أَجْرًا إِلَّا الْمَوَدَّةَ فِي الْقُرْبَىٰ ۗ وَمَن يَقْتَرِفْ حَسَنَةً نَّزِدْ لَهُ فِيهَا حُسْنًا ۚ إِنَّ اللَّهَ غَفُورٌ شَكُورٌ﴾

﴿*dhālika lladhī yubashshiru llāhu ʿibādahu lladhīna ʾāmanū wa-ʿamilū ṣ-ṣāliḥāti qul lā ʾasʾalukum ʿalayhi ʾajran ʾillā l-mawaddata fī l-qurbā wa-man yaqtarif ḥasanatan nazid lahū fīhā ḥusnan ʾinna llāha ghafūrun shakūr* ᵘⁿ﴾

﴿*That is the good news God gives to His servants who have faith and do righteous deeds!*

[57] Sūrat al-Aḥzāb, Verse 33.

Say, 'I do not ask you any reward for it except love of [my] relatives.' Whoever performs a good deed, We shall enhance for him its goodness. Indeed God is all-forgiving, all-appreciative.﴿[58]

Of course, in addition to other verses of the Qur'ān; therefore these verses and ḥadīth establish the expectation on the Islamic nation of obedience, love, and adherence to the Ahl al-Bayt ﷺ.

h. The Infallibility (*al-ʿiṣmah*) of the Imāms

The Divinely appointed leader in the view of the Imāmī Shīʿa is not an office of privilege; rather, as we said before it carries a massive responsibility that these specific exceptional individuals undertake. This responsibility cannot be taken on in its most perfect form—in the view of the Imāmīs—except by the divinely appointed leader who enjoys the highest ideals of justice and perfection. It is based on this that the Imāmīs hold the infallibility of these leaders from every sin and transgression, whether small or great, both before and after he assumes this office. This also applies for errors, mistakes, and heedlessness and they establish their own proofs for this based on reason and tradition, although there may be some difference of opinion on the details.

[58] Sūrat al-Shūrā, Verse 23.

i. Who are the Twelve Leaders?

The Divinely appointed leaders among the Imāmī Shīʿa are twelve in number—and this is a point in which they differ with the Zaydīs and Ismāʿīlīs. They are recognized either via direct attestation by the Prophet ﷺ or by attestation of the preceding Imām عليه السلام (*al-naṣṣ*). Many narrations and traditions are mentioned in the books of ḥadīth regarding the appointment of the Imāms of Ahl al-Bayt عليهم السلام based on these two methods. These twelve Imāms in order are as follows:

1. Imām ʿAlī b. Abī Ṭālib عليه السلام (*Amīr al-Mu'minīn*) (d. 40 AH)
2. Imām al-Ḥasan b. ʿAlī al-Mujtabā عليه السلام (d. 50 AH)
3. Imām al-Ḥusayn b. ʿAlī al-Shahīd عليه السلام (d. 61 AH)
4. Imām Zayn al-ʿĀbidīn عليه السلام (d. 94 AH)
5. Imām Muḥammad al-Bāqir عليه السلام (d. 114 AH)
6. Imām Jaʿfar al-Ṣādiq عليه السلام (d. 148 AH)
7. Imām Mūsā al-Kāẓim عليه السلام (d. 183 AH)
8. Imām ʿAlī al-Riḍā عليه السلام (d. 203 AH)
9. Imām Muḥammad al-Jawād عليه السلام (d. 220 AH)

10. Imām ʿAlī al-Hādī ﷵ (d. 254 AH)

11. Imām Ḥasan al-ʿAskarī ﷵ (d. 260 AH)

12. Imām Muḥammad al-Mahdī عجل الله فرجه who went into occultation and remains alive. He will emerge at the end times to fill the Earth with justice and equity after it had been filled with oppression and inequity.

In order to review the lives of these Imāms عليهم السلام, one may refer to the books of history, hadith, and biography which overflow with details on this topic: the proofs of their rank and their elevated status, their illustrious and detailed accounts, and the respect of all Muslims for them whether they be opponents or adherents.

j. Imām Mahdī عجل الله فرجه and the Belief in Mahdiology (*al-Mahdawīyyah*) and the Second Coming (*al-Rajʿah*)

The Imāmīs are unanimous currently upon belief in the Divine Leadership of the Twelfth Imām عجل الله فرجه—who is in occultation and will emerge to reform the world in the end times. The Muslims in general have also largely accepted this belief, although they differ regarding whether he has been born or not. The Imāmīs do not view his birth or his extended occultation as strange at all in light of God's ﷻ omnipotence and the existence of such a precedent in previous nations. They have discussed this issue in depth in their philosophical and historical discussions.[59]

The Imāmīs consider certain signs as precipitants to the advent of the Mahdī ﷻ and believe that with his advent, he will change the face of the Earth into a future of enlightenment and promise. They also hold that a party of those who embodied pure faith and pure disbelief will be resurrected upon his emergence for a grand confrontation to take place; this is termed in the Imāmī theology as "the Second Coming" (*al-raj'ah*). Nonetheless, there are a small group among the Imāmī scholars who interpret the Second Coming as the very advent of the Mahdī ﷻ and the return of power to the Ahl al-Bayt ﷺ and do not believe that any shall be resurrected at this time; among these scholars is Sayyid Hāshim Ma'rūf al-Ḥasanī al-'Āmilī.[60]

---

[59] For a primer regarding issues concerning Mahdiology, one may refer to the book "*Discussions Concerning al-Mahdi*" by Āyatullāh Lutfullāh Ṣāfī Golpāygāni translated by Sayyid Sulaymān Ḥasan 'Ābidi.

[60] There is some contention over the nature of the raj'ah among the Imāmiyyah, and the Lebanese scholar pointed out here by the writer is among the students of Āyatullāh Khū'ī who interpreted the ḥadīth about this topic in a metaphorical manner (see his Arabic book entitled "*al-Shī'a Bayn al-Ash'arīyah wa al-Mu'tazilah*" page 241). In English, a great analysis of the Shī'a hadith on the topic of raj'ah has been penned by Dr. Amina Inloes entitled, "*Authentication of Hadith on the Raj'ah.*"

k. The Imām's Knowledge of the Unseen (*'ilm al-ghayb*) and Cosmic Authority (*al-Wilāyah al-Takwīnīyyah*) are Disputed Areas for the Imāmīs

Just as may be expected in any sect, there are divergences among the Imāmīs in terms of the theoretical details of Imāmate. These differences can be summarized into two main points:

1. Knowledge of the unseen (*al-'ilm bi al-ghayb*): some scholars espouse that the Ahl al-Bayt 🕮 have knowledge of the unseen through direct instruction from God 🕮, not in a manner independent of Him. As such, they are privy to the esoteric aspects of creation; knowledge of the creation's deeds and continuous witnessing of their actions; knowledge of the present, past, and future until the Day of Judgement; and knowledge of all languages and scientific disciplines. They are viewed as having acquired this knowledge from God 🕮 and not at all independently of Him. They state that just as God 🕮 informed the Prophets 🕮 and apprised them of the unseen, God 🕮 did the same for the Imāms 🕮, although without making them into Prophets.

Meanwhile, this viewpoint is opposed by other scholars, who do not accept that the knowledge of the unseen granted to the Imāms 🕮 has this degree of liberality;

rather they only have a small portion of the vastness of unseen knowledge as dictated by God's ﷻ command.[61]

2. Cosmic Viceregency (*al-wilāyah al-takwīniyyah*): this implies that the Imāms ؑ have viceregency, authority, and governance of this world on account of their exalted souls and that they behave and manage its affairs through God's ﷻ command and agency. In this, they are not at all independent of Him or His omnipotence even for a moment. Their lives are inundated with marvels and cosmic interventions in the natural order that derive from the strength of their souls and psyches; their spiritual evolution has reached the highest level of ontological perfection and they are the embodiment of "The Perfect Man" (*al-insān al-kāmil*) on this planet after the Holy Prophet ﷺ.

At the same time, some Imāmī scholars refute cosmic viceregency and consider the fact that God ﷻ may at times furnish the Ahl al-Bayt ؑ with the power to influence nature due to certain exigencies or for limited

---

[61] A detailed discussion can be found about the knowledge of the Imāms in the book "*Imāmate and Leadership*" by Sayyid Mujtabā Musavī Lārī رحمه الله, specifically under Lessons 20 and 21. Among the Shī'a scholars who have advocated for the view that the Imāms had very limited knowledge of the unseen was the late Āyatullāh Ni'matullāh Ṣālchī Najafābādī رحمه الله. His work about this was translated to English by Dr. Ḥamīd Mavānī and is entitled "*Religious Extremism: Intellectual and Doctrinal Deviance in Islam.*"

moments. Nonetheless, they do not manage the world or reckon the deeds of creation; their lives did not operate on the basis of miracles and marvels, but rather were quite ordinary most of the time.

A faction of the Imāmīs and their scholars in the present-day adopt the position of refuting these two viewpoints (knowledge of the unseen and the cosmic viceregency) and their related concepts. It is possible for one to review these topics in the books of Shīʿa theology.[62]

In any case, Imāmate is a natural consequence of the Muḥammadan prophethood and therefore all the characteristics that the Imāmī Shīʿa confirm for the Imāms naturally exist at an even higher level of perfection for the Messenger of God, Prophet Muḥammad ﷺ. Therefore, when Imāmīs claim that the Imām has knowledge of the unseen, they believe that the Prophet ﷺ also has knowledge of the unseen, rather to a level even more pristine and complete, being as he is the most perfected of creation and the most elevated in rank with God ﷻ.

---

62 Much of the discussion on this frontier is present mostly in non-English sources. However, for a good introduction and discussion of these theological matters one may refer to the book "*Shīʿīsm, Imāmate, and Wilāyat*" by Sayyid Muḥammad Rizvī.

The Fourth Axis: The Afterlife (*al-Ma'ād*) and the Resurrection (*al-Qiyāmah*)

The Imāmīs have a deep and unshakeable conviction in the Day of Judgement, considering it definitively a rational requirement and a Divine Promise. It is the Day of Ultimate Justice and the manifestation of the Supreme Divine Omnipotence where humankind is resurrected for reckoning in front of God ﷻ. This resurrection is in both body and spirit, being as how there is no room for acceptance of the belief in reincarnation (*al-tanāsukh*) that is accepted by some religions and creeds. The popular belief among the Imāmī scholars is the existence of the world of the grave (*'ālam al-qabr*): either for all people or for a select few of those who embodied pure faith (such as the martyrs) or those who embodied pure disbelief (such as Pharaoh and his people). The realm of the grave (*al-barzakh*) is among those affairs in which great controversy has arisen, as its denial has been attributed to some Muslims such as Ḍirār b. ʿAmr.[63]

The Imāmīs believe—as other Muslims—in the signs and conditions of Armageddon (*ʿalāmāt al-sāʿah*) that must occur for its actualization. Additionally, they accept the manifestations of the Day of Judgement as they are alluded to in Sūrat al-Takwīr, Sūrat al-Infiṭār, Sūrat al-Inshiqāq, Sūrat al-Zalzalah, and Sūrat al-Qāriʿah. Among the conditions of Armageddon are the following: the manifest smoke (*al-dukhān al-mubīn*), the return of Christ (*nuzūl al-masīḥ*), the emergence of the creature of the Earth (*khurūj dābbat al-arḍ*) among

---

[63] Ḍirār b. ʿAmr al-Ghaṭafānī al-Baṣrī (d. 215 AH) was one of the chief theologians among the Muʿtazilah. He interpreted verses of the Qurʾān very literally to refute the idea of the barzakh such as the following,

﴿لَا يَذُوقُونَ فِيهَا الْمَوْتَ إِلَّا الْمَوْتَةَ الْأُولَىٰ﴾

﴿*lā yadhūqūna fīhā l-mawta ʾillā l-mawtata l-ʾūlā*﴾

﴿*There they will not taste death except the first death*﴾

Sūrat al-Dukhān, Verse 56.

For further details on the Shīʿa belief about barzakh and a theological refutation of the arguments made against its existence, one may refer to the book "Barzakh (Purgatory)" by Āyatullāh Sayyid ʿAbdul Ḥusayn Dastghayb Shirāzī.

others that are mentioned although there may be some divergence in details.[64]

The Day of Judgement in the Imāmī conception passes through the initial stage of the first blowing of the trumpet (*nafkh al-ṣūr*), whereby all creation dies; then the second blowing of the trumpet whereby they are all resurrected; the third stage whereby they are presented their deeds for them to witness (*ʿarḍ al-aʿamāl*); then their reckoning whereby they are held accountable for every deed while witnesses testify against them, including the Prophets, the angels, the Earth, their bodies, and their flesh. After this reckoning, many of the Imāmī scholars adopt the view of a bridge (*al-ṣirāṭ*) over Hell that people are made to pass over: sharper than a sword and thinner than a single strand of hair; whoever is successful in reckoning traverses it, whereas those who do not fall into the pit of Hell.[65]

By the same token, the Imāmī scholars believe in the Divine Veiling (*al-ḥijāb*) and the Heights (*al-Aʿarāf*), whereby individuals whom the traditions make clear are the Prophets and their successors will stand. The Imāmī

---

[64] An excellent overview of the signs of Resurrection can be found in the book "*Resurrection (Maʿād) in the Qur'ān*," by Āyatullāh Ibrāhīm Amīnī translated by Sayyid Athar Husayn Rizvi.

[65] Of note, this belief is not unique to the Imāmī Shīʿa. Ahl al-Sunnah also has similar descriptions about al-Ṣirāṭ narrated in their ḥadīth collections of Bukhārī and Muslim.

traditions also allude to the fact that after reckoning, the Prophet ﷺ will carry the banner of praise (*liwāʾ al-ḥamd*) and enter Heaven, after which the believers will enter in his wake.[66]

The recompense on the Day of Judgement is either Heaven or Hell; however, prior to admittance to Hell it is possible for intercession (*al-shafāʿah*) to overtake an individual. The implication of this doctrine is that some of the choicest with God ﷻ are able to intercede for

---

[66] These beliefs are again shared by all Muslims. The veil referred to here is the one that will separate the people of Heaven from the people of Hell as described in the following verse of the Qurʾān:

﴿وَبَيْنَهُمَا حِجَابٌ ۚ وَعَلَى الْأَعْرَافِ رِجَالٌ يَعْرِفُونَ كُلًّا بِسِيمَاهُمْ ۚ وَنَادَوْا
أَصْحَابَ الْجَنَّةِ أَنْ سَلَامٌ عَلَيْكُمْ ۚ لَمْ يَدْخُلُوهَا وَهُمْ يَطْمَعُونَ﴾

﴿*wa-baynahumā ḥijābun wa-ʿalā l-ʾaʿrāfi rijālun yaʿrifūna kullan bi-sīmāhum wa-nādaw ʾaṣḥāba l-jannati ʾan salāmun ʿalaykum lam yadkhulūhā wa-hum yaṭmaʿūn* [a]﴾

﴿*And there will be a veil between them. And on the Elevations will be certain men who recognize each of them by their mark. They will call out to the inhabitants of paradise, 'Peace be to you!' (They* will not have entered it, though they would be eager to do so.*﴾

* That is, the people of paradise.

Sūrat al-Aʿrāf, Verse 46.

some Muslims within certain limits prescribed by God ﷻ, and the most prominent of all such folk are Prophet Muḥammad ﷺ and his Ahl al-Bayt ﷻ. Hence, there is no harm in seeking the intercession of these individuals even while in this world, just as the sons of Jacob also sought from their father to intercede for them:

﴿قَالُوا يَا أَبَانَا اسْتَغْفِرْ لَنَا ذُنُوبَنَا إِنَّا كُنَّا خَاطِئِينَ﴾

﴿qālū yā-'abānā staghfir lanā dhunūbanā 'innā kunnā khāṭi'īn a﴾

﴿قَالَ سَوْفَ أَسْتَغْفِرُ لَكُمْ رَبِّيٓ إِنَّهُ هُوَ الْغَفُورُ الرَّحِيمُ﴾

﴿qāla sawfa 'astaghfiru lakum rabbī 'innahū huwa l-ghafūru r-raḥīm u﴾

﴿They said, 'Father! Plead [with God] for forgiveness of our sins! We have indeed been erring.' He said, 'I shall plead with my Lord to forgive you; indeed He is the All-forgiving, the All-merciful.'﴾[67]

Now intercession is not at all subject to arbitrariness (*fawḍā*) or nepotism (*maḥsūbīyyāt*); rather it has its own governing laws that are not actualized except with the pleasure of God ﷻ in order that he may bestow to

[67] Sūrat Yūsuf, Verses 97-98.

the interceders their proper station on the Day of Judgement.

The reckoning of God ﷻ on the Day of Judgement is just, without any oppression: the human being is held accountable for every small or great sin, however if he repented to God ﷻ then He wipes it away from his account; or he may receive intercession from those endowed with this faculty; or he may be engulfed by the general mercy of God.

Indeed, God ﷻ—The Most Forgiving—pardons all sins if one seeks repentance (*al-tawbah*) and may even forgive sins on His own discretion without repentance excepting associating partners with Him (*al-shirk*).

The Noble Qur'ān documents this in God's ﷻ words:

﴿إِنَّ اللَّهَ لَا يَغْفِرُ أَنْ يُشْرَكَ بِهِ وَيَغْفِرُ مَا دُونَ ذَٰلِكَ لِمَنْ يَشَاءُ ۚ وَمَنْ يُشْرِكْ بِاللَّهِ فَقَدِ افْتَرَىٰ إِثْمًا عَظِيمًا﴾

﴿*'inna llāha lā yaghfiru 'an yushraka bihī wa-yaghfiru mā dūna dhālika li-man yashā'u wa-man yushrik bi-llāhi fa-qadi ftarā 'ithman ʿaẓīma* ^{n}﴾

﴾*Indeed God does not forgive that any partner should be ascribed to Him, but He forgives anything besides that to whomever He wishes. And whoever ascribes partners to God has indeed fabricated [a lie] in great sinfulness.*﴿[68]

Similarly, God ﷻ states in another excerpt of the Qur'ān:

﴿قُلْ يَا عِبَادِيَ الَّذِينَ أَسْرَفُوا عَلَىٰ أَنفُسِهِمْ لَا تَقْنَطُوا مِن رَّحْمَةِ اللَّهِ ۚ إِنَّ اللَّهَ يَغْفِرُ الذُّنُوبَ جَمِيعًا ۚ إِنَّهُ هُوَ الْغَفُورُ الرَّحِيمُ﴾

﴾*qul yā-'ibādiya lladhīna 'asrafū 'alā 'anfusihim lā taqnaṭū min raḥmati llāhi 'inna llāha yaghfiru dh-dhunūba jamī'an 'innahū huwa l-ghafūru r-raḥīm*﴿

﴾Say *[that God declares,] 'O My servants who have committed excesses against their own souls, do not despair of the mercy of God. Indeed God will forgive all sins. Indeed He is the All-forgiving, the All-merciful.*﴿[69]

If none of these three things actualize (i.e., repentance, intercession, or mercy), then the servant becomes worthy of Hell, although permanence in it is limited only to disbelieving idolaters, not monotheistic Muslims.

---

[68] Sūrat al-Nisā', Verse 48.

[69] Sūrat al-Zumar, Verse 53.

This is a brief sketch of the most important and widespread beliefs of the Imāmī sect, although there are some supplementary details subject to controversy and dispute within the sect and outside of it that there is no need at this juncture to discuss.

The Precepts of Sharīʿah Among the Imāmī Shīʿa

The Imāmīs—as other Muslims—believe in a complete Islamic sharīʿah and hold that it is the most pristine system of governance founded for humankind. They believe that if one were to stay adherent to the guidance of the Islamic Sharīʿa, all his affairs would be remedied. Furthermore, they hold that among the most pressing reasons for the abjectness of the Muslim condition lies in their distance from religion and implementing God's ﷻ law. The belief of the Imāmīs in sharīʿah is embodied in the selfsame jurisprudential matters known by all Muslims: ablution (*al-wuḍūʾ*), ritual bath (*al-ghusl*), dry ablution (*al-tayammum*), ritual purity and impurity (*al-ṭahārāt wa al-najāsāt*), prayers (*al-ṣalāt*), fasting (*al-ṣawm*), pilgrimage (*al-ḥajj*), alms-giving (*al-zakāt*), spiritual retreat (*al-iʿtikāf*), enjoining good (*al-amr bi al-maʿrūf*), forbidding evil (*al-nahy ʿan al-munkar*), the one-fifth tax (*al-khums*), combat in God's ﷻ way (*al-jihād*), rules of trade and rent (*aḥkām al-bayʿ wa al-ijārah*), marriage (*al-nikāḥ*), divorce (*al-ṭalāq*), imprecation (*al-liʿān*), freeing slaves (*al-ʿitq*), swears/

oaths/covenants (*al-aymān wa al-nudhūr wa al-ʿuhūd*), expiation (*al-kaffārāt*), revocation (*al-iqālah*), pre-emption (*al-shufʿah*), profit sharing (*al-muḍārabah*), sharecropping (*al-muzāraʿah wa al-musāqāt*), war preparation (*al-sabq wa al-rimāyah*), trade partnership (*al-shirkah*), deposit (*al-wadīʿah*), borrowing (*al-ʿāriyah*), lost property (*al-luqaṭah*), usurpation (*al-ghaṣb*), revival of dead lands (*iḥyāʾ al-mawāt*), public dominion (*al-mushtarakāt*), debt (*al-dayn*), loaning (*al-qarḍ*), mortgage (*al-rahn*), asset suspension (*al-hajar*), warranty (*al-ḍamān*), contract law (*al-ṣulḥ*), donation (*al-hibah*), calling wives as mothers (*al-ẓihār*), abstinence oaths (*al-īlāʾ*), inheritance (*al-irth*), bequeathment (*al-waṣiyyah*), endowment (*al-waqf*), charity (*al-ṣadaqah*), commission (*al-juʿālah*), debt transference (*al-ḥawālah*), guarantee (*al-kafālah*), contractual agency (*al-wakālah*), capital punishments (*al-ḥudūd*), retaliation (*al-qiṣāṣ*), discretionary punishments (*al-taʿzīrāt*), ransoms (*al-diyāt*), arbitration (*al-qaḍāʾ*), testimony (*al-shahādāt*), confession (*al-iqrār*), hunting (*al-ṣayd*), slaughter (*al-dhabāḥah*), food and drink (*al-aṭʿimah wa al-ashribah*), modesty and glancing at the opposite gender (*al-satr wa al-naẓar*), gender relations (*al-ʿalāqah bayn al-jinsayn*), guardianship (*al-wilāyah*), etc.

Those who review the books of the Imāmīs regarding this will not find many significant differences between them and those of the books of other Muslims; rather they are nearly identical jurisprudentially.[70]

The Sources of Jurisprudential Reasoning Among the Imāmīs

In reference to the derivation of religious edicts, the Imāmīs rely on the Qur'ān, the Prophetic tradition (al-sunnah), the traditions of the Ahl al-Bayt ﷺ (seen as a commentary on the Qur'ān and the Prophetic traditions); and rationality (*al-ʿaql*; although there is some divergence between them on this). As for consensus (*al-ijmāʿ*), the Imāmīs view it as revelatory of the Prophetic tradition but not as evidence for its content.[71]

[70] Those interested in seeing the layout of Shīʿa jurisprudence on this topic may consider reviewing the collections of fatāwā of some of the great modern-day religious authorities in Twelver Imāmī Shīʿism, such as Āyatullāh Sayyid ʿAli Sistānī's "*Islāmic Laws*".

[71] The meaning here is that when the early Islāmic community had a consensus on a certain practice, it implies that an oral proof must have existed at that time to substantiate it even if it is extinct now. Therefore, consensus is not used as a source of sharīʿah per se; rather it is used to substantiate that a part of the sunnah that is no longer extant in today's sources must have existed upon which the early scholars had based their view, even if it was not transmitted to us. For more details regarding this issue and more insight into Shīʿa fiqh, please refer to the excellent text "*Jurisprudence and its Principles*" by Āyatullāh Murtaḍā Muṭahharī ؒ, translated by Muḥammad Salmān Tawhīdī.

The Imāmī Shīʿa do not believe in analogical reasoning (*al-qiyās*), juristic discretion (*al-istiḥsān*), or the institution of scholarly opinion (*madrasah al-ra'y*). However, there are still a number of jurisprudential and methodological differences between them as with every other Muslim jurisprudential school, the most principal being the difference between the rationalists (*al-uṣūliyīn*) and traditionists (*al-akhbāriyīn*).[72]

The majority Imāmī opinion distinguishes itself from the majority of other schools of Muslim fiqh in a number of juridical rulings (*al-aḥkām*) that we enumerate as below:

a. The necessity of emulation of a living juristic authority (*al-marjaʿ*) considered at the highest level of expertise (*al-aʿlam*) in the branches of jurisprudence.

b. The necessity of wiping the feet (*al-masḥ*) in ablution instead of washing them (*al-ghusl*).

c. The invalidity of prostration (*al-sujūd*) on anything which can be eaten or worn.

[72] For a detailed overview about Akhbārism and Uṣūlism, please refer to the book "*The Principle of Ijtihād in Islām*" by Āyatullāh Murtaḍā Muṭahharī ؒ, translated by John Cooper.

d. The permissibility of combining the mid-day prayer (*al-ẓuhr*) with the afternoon prayer (*al-ʿaṣr*) and combining the evening prayer (*al-maghrib*) and the night prayer (*al-ʿishāʾ*) at all times without any exigency or travel

e. The acceptability of temporary marriage (*al-mutʿah*)

f. The invalidity of folding one's hands (*al-takattuf*) while in the standing position of prayers

g. The invalidity of praying in congregation (*al-jamāʿah*) in the supererogatory prayers (*al-nawāfil*)[73]

h. The applicability of the one-fifth tax on personal earnings (*arbāḥ al-makāsib*), not only on war booty and treasures

i. The prohibition on saying "Amen" (*al-taʾmīn*) in prayers as a recommended act after reciting the chapter of The Opening (*al-Fātiḥah*).

[73] This is a specific reference to the prayers of tarāwīḥ that are done in Ramaḍān, whereby Sunnīs will pray in congregation and listen to the recitation of the whole Qurʾān behind an imām.

j. The lack of necessity for witnesses in marriage (*al-nikāḥ*) while prescribing the necessity of witnesses for divorce (*al-ṭalāq*)

k. The inability to annul a marriage thrice (*al-ṭalāqāt al-thalāth*) in a single setting; rather one can only annul a marriage once in a given setting.

l. The permissibility of switching in pilgrimage from the ʿumrah to the ḥajj (*al-tamattuʿ*).

m. The rejection of mutual diminishment and estate sharing in reference to inheritance (*al-ʿawl wa al-taʿṣīb*)

n. The necessity of stating "Come to the best of deeds" in the first and second calls to prayer (*al-adhān wa al-iqāmah*) and the impermissibility of saying "Prayer is better than sleep."

Among other examples of juristic variance that we will not delve into deeply here.

In that Case, Why the Differences?

From the discussion that preceded, it has become clear that the Shīʿa Imāmī sect is an Islamic one that believes in the entirety of Islamic theology and divine law; the core principles of creed and jurisprudence do not differ significantly from the Muslim orthodoxy. Rather, whenever there is a divergence in Imāmite doctrine, a parallel schism can be drawn within Muslim orthodoxy as well.

The question therefore is why the variances between the four major Sunnī juridical schools have been resolved while the relationship with the Imāmī sect has remained tense and turbulent? Why has the Muslim orthodoxy come to accept theological differences in belief among themselves (for instance, consider the *Māturīdī*, *Muʿtazilite*, and *Ashʿarite* schools) despite their enormity, while the differences with the Imāmite sect have received an altogether different and more unwelcoming stance?

Moreover, the juristic differences between the four Sunnī schools of law suffer from hundreds of differences and controversial religious edicts (*al-fatāwā*) across the board; therefore, what is it that has rendered the differences with the Imāmī juristic school strained within the Sunnī psyche while all these variances within their own schools have not created the same level of tension?

In our modern-day era, the Muʿtazilites, Ashʿarites, Maturidis, and literalists (*ahl al-ḥadīth*) —with the exception of the Salafīs— all live in harmony and consider themselves under the auspices of the single sect of Ahl al-Sunnah despite the intensity of criticism and variation between them. Therefore, why have the Imāmī-Sunnī relations not assumed the same form of mutual appreciation of differences and assimilation? What is the issue and why is there this perception that the Imāmī Shīʿa, who constitute more than 200 million Muslims in the world, are outside the framework of the Islamic creed?

There are no doubt disconcerting elements that need to be eradicated in order that we may return back to the shade of unity in spite of diversity and agreement in the midst of disagreement, without yielding to excommunicatory rhetoric. A thorough examination of these elements of tension and anxiety is therefore the key to the solution for this topic; therefore, what are these elements and what are the most prominent among them? This is what we will endeavor to address now, after which we will proceed to establish the foundations of managing our differences, God willing.

The Difference of Today is Between the Imāmīs and Some Muslims, not All of Them

It is imperative that I point out that in the current circumstance, we do not face a crisis of relations between the Imāmīs and all other Islamic sects; this is an incorrect statement given that the Imāmīs actually have very good relationships with the Zaydīs in Yemen, the Ibāḍīs in Oman, the Ismāʿīlīs in the Indian and Arabian subcontinents, and the Ṣūfīs in Pakistan, India, and

North Africa. Rather, the core problem lies with the majority of Ahl al-Sunnah with their theological and juristic schools—and in particular with the Salafī movement.

The Shīʿa and the Sunnah: Mutual Concepts and Related Issues

Introduction

We all recognize that since the earliest centuries after the Hijrah, the Sunnīs and Shīʿas have had many a difference, although the main issue is not in difference of thought but rather in the psychological barriers that have stood in the face of mutual collaboration. This is the grave conundrum in our relationship: namely, the existence of phenomena, behaviors, and persuasions that sometimes leak into religious and sectarian discourse and render it impossible to establish harmony and religious tolerance. Among these are the following:

a. The declaration of heresy (*al-takfīr*) that some Muslims cast on the Imāmī Shīʿas on the basis of polytheism and intercession (*al-tawassul)*; i.e., a failure to recognize religious difference

b. Cursing the Prophet's ﷺ companions (*laʿn al-ṣaḥābah*)

c. Belittling and attacking the Mothers of the Believers (*ummahāt al-mu'minīn*)

d. Dissimulation (*al-taqīyyah*)

e. The Distortion (*al-taḥrīf*) of the Noble Qur'ān and the Rejection of the Prophetic Tradition

f. 'Āshūrā' and its Associated Ceremonies and Rituals

g. Temporary Marriage (*al-mut'ah*)

h. Shī'a Expansionism (*al-madd al-shī'ī*)

i. Quashing of Religious Freedom (*qam' al-ḥurrīyyāt al-madhhabīyyah*)

Among many other issues that assume critical importance and intervene in our mutual collaboration. It is necessary to examine these issues in detail and render a position in order to establish the foundations of a new state of relations.

The Issue of Excommunication (*al-takfīr*) and Accusing Others of Polytheism (*al-shirk*)

This issue presents itself as one of the most complicated problems that challenges the Muslims' peaceful convergence as some sectarian currents among the Ahl al-Sunnah—the Salafīs in particular—insist on considering the Imāmīs as disbelievers (*kuffār*) and idolaters (*mushrikīn*) due to their stance in reference to graves and their relationship with the Imāms of the Ahl al-Bayt عليهم السلام. This stubbornness has reached a level whereby even some groups among the Ahl al-Sunnah such as the Ṣūfīs and the spiritualists (*al-rūḥiyyah*) have not been spared.

The Imāmīs have defended themselves in this regard and explained their stance, however we do not intend to epistemologically dissect this issue here;[74] rather we will instead render our conclusions on this issue: what we consider essential here is disposing of the language of accusing others of heresy (*al-takfīr*) and revising it from the ground up, such that one does not judge a whole sect on the basis of some actions and words adopted by a small faction from amongst that sect. We must open the horizon of assuming the best of others (*ḥusn al-ẓann*) in reference to their practices and actions and should not stereotype a sect based on a specific inflexible interpretation.

The Gravity of Excommunication

We seek that takfīr be deemed a grave and dangerous affair, impermissible except in extenuating circumstances; it should be the responsibility of the grand jurists and learned jurisprudents (*al-mujtahidīn*) in the Muslim community to declare such a statement. Similarly, it should also be their responsibility to have

---

[74] For a detailed scholarly rebuttal of the Salafī objections, please refer to the work of Āyatullāh Ja'far Subḥānī titled "*Wahhābism*," edited and revised by Aḥmad 'Abdullah Martin.

extreme reservation in allowing just any given individual to release religious edicts (*al-fatāwā*), as the chaos that ensues from arbitrary use of this agency from undeserving folks without supervision or censorship has and will lead to pandemonium in the appraisal of others' orthodoxy/heresy.

In the same breath, we also seek that some among the Imāmī Shīʿa abandon this practice of takfīr—even if implicit—in reference to other sects. We have found several efforts among the Shīʿas and Sunnīs that have adopted the stance of accepting the Muslim status of all Islamic sects, both effectively and nominally, and we view it appropriate that these efforts become the officially accepted stance in the general culture. Of course, freedom of opinion and differing scholarly views can be accommodated for religious conferences and inter-sectarian discourse without triggering a crisis in the relationship between Muslims.

Calling The Imāmīs Towards Reforming Certain Practices

Since many of those who accuse the Imāmīs of disbelief predicate their claims upon false conceptions regarding our reckoning of the status of the Ahl al-Bayt عليهم السلام, we appeal to the Shīʿa Marjaʿīyyah to critique the incorrect practices—perpetrated by the minority—that distort the image of the Imāmī creed in front of others. Indeed, these types of actions only add fuel to the fire in justifying the culture of takfīr.

We therefore repudiate these practices that are unnecessary and have no sufficient evidence to mandate or encourage them, such as prostration in front of shrines, the custom of directing supplication towards a saint (*ṣāhib al-ḍarīḥ*) instead of God ﷻ, and the custom of calling out to saints for assistance. Examples that may be cited include calling out "Oh ʿAlī!" when standing or sitting and the supplication: "Oh Muḥammad, Oh ʿAlī! Oh ʿAlī, Oh Muḥammad! Assist me as you are my two assistants and suffice me as you two are sufficient!"[75] Instead, we call towards returning to the Qurʾānic duʿās, the duʿās of al-Sahīfah al-Sajjādīyyah, and the well-founded duʿas of the Ahl al-Bayt ﷺ found in both Shīʿa and Sunnī ḥadīth collections.

Our Conception of the Issue of Intercession (*al-tawassul*) in the Prophet ﷺ and Saints (*al-awliyāʾ*)

This is our conception of the doctrine of tawassul: we therefore appeal to our Shīʿa brethren to abstain from the type of tawassul that takes the form of supplication towards the Ahl al-Bayt ﷺ or others as though they fulfill the needs of the people. Rather, we perceive this as a weak deduction based on sources that are few and

[75] Al-Mashhadi, *Al-Mazār Al-Kabīr*, Vol. 2, p. 591.

far between. Moreover, we view it as being irreconcilable with the general compendium of supplications bequeathed to us from the Ahl al-Bayt 🕮.[76]

Instead, we believe in tawassul in the sense of turning towards God 🕮 and invoking Him to grant a request for the sake of Muḥammad 🕮, his progeny 🕮, the Prophets 🕮 (al-nabiyyīn), the saints (al-awliyā'), the paragons of truth (al-ṣiddīqīn), the martyrs (al-shuhadā'), and the righteous (al-ṣāliḥīn)—indeed how glorious a company![77]

We do not find any inkling of polytheism in this rather it is pure monotheism, for one is approaching the vicinity of His presence while invoking the reputation of the Prophets and the righteous.

---

[76] It should be noted that Ḥubbullah is not alone in this view; rather even other scholars like Āyatullāh Faḍlullāh 🕮 and Āyatullāh Muṭahharī 🕮 have supported this approach of using tawassul instead of istighāthah (i.e., direct invocation of the Ahl al-Bayt 🕮). For a detailed view on this topic, one may refer to the chapter on Intercession in Āyatullāh Murtaḍā Muṭahharī's "Divine Justice" translated by Sayyid Sulaymān Ḥasan Ābidī, Shaykh Murtazā Alidina, and Shaykh Shujaʿ Alī Mirza. It should be noted that this is a controversial issue and there are other scholars who have voiced unswerving support for istighāthah such as Āyatullāh Jaʿfar Subḥānī and Sayyid Kamāl al-Ḥaydarī.

[77] This is an allusion to Sūrat al-Nisāʾ, Verse 69.

Calling the Ahl al-Sunnah Towards Understanding Their Fellow Muslims

Our invitation to the Shīʿa is as aforementioned, while our call to the Sunnī brethren is to seek to understand and reliably ascertain what actually occurs at the shrines. They should abstain from entertaining the blatant exaggerations that seek to misconstrue the Shīʿa creed as polytheism or disbelief (we seek only God's ﷻ protection from such calumny). The Shīʿa are no doubt pure monotheist Muslims, and even if they do espouse a certain station or rank for the Ahl al-Bayt عليهم السلام in this world they believe it is strictly of God's ﷻ bounties upon them and is not at all independent of Him. Their parable is like that of the Sun, which provides life to the Earth through the authorization of God ﷻ: it is certainly not a deity to be worshipped beside Him and is never separated from His will in carrying out the role He has assigned to it.

Cosmic Authority (*al-Wilāyah al-Takwīnīyyah*) and the Question of Shirk: Correcting Misconceptions

In fact, the above is also exactly what is espoused by those who assign cosmic authority and knowledge of the unseen to the Imāms عليهم السلام. Although we do not agree with them on this point, they nonetheless do not seek to deify anyone and there is no implication of such in their theory. They do not believe in a doctrine of God ﷻ

being deficient and requiring the Ahl al-Bayt عليهم السلام to fill His inadequacy; neither do they hold that God ﷿ requires the assistance of anyone; neither do they believe that He has relegated (*al-tafwīḍ*) management of His universe to the Ahl al-Bayt عليهم السلام! Such beliefs are abominable and are considered heretical—rather many of the Imāmī jurists considered the heretics as disbelievers and ritually unclean.

The crux of their conception is that God ﷿ informs the Ahl al-Bayt عليهم السلام of the unseen while they themselves have no power to know even an iota of the ghayb without Him. In the same token, if they have any cosmic authority over the universe then this is solely through God's ﷿ empowerment—just as how He has empowered me to use this pen to write on these blank pages. Therefore, the Ahl al-Bayt عليهم السلام only received this faculty from God ﷿ and are completely dependent on Him in perpetuity (*ḥudūthan*) and continuously (*istimrāran*); were He to remove His Providence then they would not persist as such for even a moment.

Hence, there is no reason to invoke takfīr on this basis even if we should view this belief as inherently erroneous; for errancy is one thing while declaring one a disbeliever and a polytheist is a different matter altogether!

Calling Towards Understanding Prostration on Ḥusaynī Soil (*al-turbah al-ḥusayniyyah*) and Visitation of Mausoleums

At this juncture, the question of prostration on Ḥusaynī clay arises. It does not imply at all worship of the clay and no Shīʿa would ever claim such a thing. In fact, the only belief here is that prostration on clay is preferable and that the clay which is honored to carry the purified corpse of the Master of the Martyrs—Imām al-Ḥusayn ﷺ—is the best of clay. Therefore, the Shīʿa prefer prostration on clay derived from this location; it has nothing to do with worship of the clay (we seek God's ﷻ protection). In other words, prostration on clay is analogous to turning towards the blessed qiblah: it does not imply worship of the method.

It should be said that the Shīʿa Imāmīs do not consider it obligatory or incumbent at all to prostrate on clay derived from Karbalāʾ or its shrine. The same applies also to visitation of the gravesites of the Prophetic family—its visitation does not at all imply worship rather it is just as the visitation of Makkah or Madīnah. Among the Imāmīs it is only for the sake of obeying God ﷻ in His commanding the preservation of relations with his saints and pious deputies—now where is the polytheism in this?!

The Crisis of Excommunication and The Repercussion of Such Actions

The problem with takfīr lies in casting the judgement of disbelief based on the implication latent in the words of another: when a person adopts a certain thought, we may label him as a disbeliever because this thought entails another thought that carries the import of disbelief. However, we fail to realize that it does not follow that the opposing party disbelieves—for perhaps he does not believe that his initial thought entails the second premise! This is indeed a great calamity pervasive in the practice of takfīr among Muslims. The biggest mistake committed by Muslims in dealing with other sects and those of dissenting viewpoints lies in holding them by the exigencies of their own sect as if the opposing party believes in these exigencies. Indeed, this is one of the cornerstone fallacies of takfīr and the declaration of apostasy.

As an example, the Sunnī tells the Shīʿa, "You stand against the Prophet ﷺ as a direct consequence of the fact that you try to break our link with him in cutting out the intermediary of the companions (*al-Ṣaḥābah*)." Meanwhile, the Shīʿa says, "This deduction you have made is not correct, because I have another intermediary (i.e. the Ahl al-Bayt ﵈), and I do not believe that my stance about the companions leads to the conclusion that you surmise."

The Necessity of Confining Issues of Excommunication to Only the Most Senior Scholars of the Ummah

Another major fallacy lies in the fact that immature scholars—rather even some of those amongst the laity without adequate training in religious sciences and the nuances of takfīr and apostasy—have assumed the reins in casting aspersions of takfīr. They do so without any ability to differentiate one sect from another and without any method of ascertaining the belief of others; what a grave danger! Instead, the matter of takfīr requires extensive expertise and intellectual struggle from the most senior scholars and jurists of the Islamic world. It should not be left by any means to the more junior scholars, those among the laity who deliver khuṭbahs or appear on television channels—doing takfīr while not comprehensively studying the religious and legal sciences. The issue of which sect is being castigated and which sect is castigating is completely a secondary issue to this discussion.

The Stance Towards the Companions (*al-Ṣaḥābah*) and the Mothers of the Believers (*Ummahāt al-Mu'minīn*)

If the aforementioned topics of tawḥīd and shirk are considered one of the greatest points of contention between the Imāmīyyah and Salafīyyah, then the subject of the companions of the Prophet is an even more grave issue, as it is a point of contention between the Imāmīyyah and the Sunnī community at large. We will briefly mention a few points regarding this topic, addressing members of both Shīʿa and Sunnī sects:

Refusal to Strip (*al-Muṣādarah*) the Right of Ijtihād in Issues of History

As we have stated before and will continue to emphasize, we believe that every Muslim has the right to do ijtihād in the various religious discussions that fall under the umbrella of the two testimonies (*al-shahādatayn*) that comprise the greater Islam. Among the most pertinent of these religious questions are the historical ones; Islamic history is a ripe field for academic study and a source of myriad opinions and approaches exist for its analysis and understanding.

As such, we do not find it logical for one side to revoke the right of another party in their understanding and analysis of history. We ask our Sunnī brethren to revise their tabooing the possibility of errancy on the part of the companions; if an individual should perform ijtihād and come to the conclusion that some of the companions did indeed make errors, there is no harm in this opinion whether we agree with their conclusions or not. In order to arrive at some degree of agreement, it is upon the Ahl al-Sunnah to open the door of ijtihād in history and in particular matters related to the first-century hijrī and what transpired between the companions. Likewise, it is upon the Shīʿa to allow other Muslims to do ijtihād in matters of history as well in reference to the history of the Imāms and the Shīʿa scholars.

This is the key to reeling in this issue away from a chaotic trajectory back on the track of appropriate academic investigation; everyone subordinate to the Holy Prophet ﷺ has been a subject of dispute amongst the Muslims. Hence the principle of ʿadālah of all companions is disagreed upon by the Imāmīyyah, and the concept of Imāmah is disagreed upon by the Sunnīs. As long as these areas remain a point of contention, there is no reason to be inimical against them; rather the way to deal with such issues is only through academic engagement.

The matter of history is key to understanding Islam and it is necessary that we all contemplate over this history with credible methods and tools of investigation.

Between the Mistakes of the Companions and Accusations of Kufr

Secondly, when a Shīʿī does ijtihād in the matter of the companions—predicated on lack of his belief in absolute justice of all companions, let alone their infallibility—and arrives at the conclusion that errors were perpetrated by them, then does this conclusion truly imply they have committed an act of disbelief (*kufr*)?

No matter how much your viewpoint insists that the Shīʿa are in error, their mistaken belief does not mean they are disbelievers. Even if you believe the Qurʾān clearly stipulates ʿadālah of the companions, others may not understand nor interpret those verses to be conclusive evidence for the integrity of all companions. As long as that is the case, you cannot accuse them of holding a position 'against the Qurʾān', let alone against the Prophet ﷺ.

It is necessary to always differentiate between a mistaken conclusion and disbelief, conspiracy, enmity, or any other similar charge. Otherwise, in every historical matter or issue of theology wherein there happens to be a dispute, one party would be accused of disbelief and eventually nothing will be left of the Muslim ummah.

It is truly an enigma that some render negatively the Imāmī Shīʿī view of the infallibility of the Ahl al-Bayt عليهم السلام, arguing that there are no sacred figures in Islam; this is while they themselves, without even realizing, ascribe sanctity to tens and thousands of companions. So if you conduct ijtihād in the matter of the companions and consider them as possessing a certain extent of sanctity – and we respect your ijtihād – then leave others to conducting their own ijtihād in the matter of their

Imāms, as per reliance on their evidence. It is not appropriate for any group to excommunicate or slander another just because they believe in the sanctity of a certain individual.

It is also necessary for us all to acknowledge that the fact some companions were mistaken is not a matter only found in the Imāmī books of ḥadīth and history. It is not the case that the Shīʿa just have a penchant for criticizing the companions; rather if we but only reflected, we would see that the Shīʿa themselves rely upon and resort to tens of sources and works of the Ahl al-Sunnah to form this conclusion.[78] This reveals that the ḥadīth and historical heritage of all Muslims do contain such discourse regarding the companions, which once again should allow one to grant greater room for accepting the ijtihād of others on this matter.

The Imāmī Corpus (*al-turāth al-imāmi*) and the Question of the Companions

Thirdly, just as we have invited the Sunnīs to revisit their positions, we also invite the Imāmī Shīʿa to calmly revisit their understanding of the companions of the

---

[78] As an example, see the report known as the *Ḥadīth al-Ḥawḍ* which indicates that at least some of the companions were misguided after the Prophet ﷺ and did not remain in the same state that the Prophet ﷺ had left them in.

Prophet ﷺ, putting aside all remnants of historical and sectarian tensions. Is it the case that some of the decisions made by some of the companions were planned conspiracy, disbelief, and apostasy? Or perhaps it was merely a mistake and a lapse in judgement or ijtihād? Is it really the case that all the companions disbelieved—as some have opined—except a few companions that one can count on one hand?[79]

The Shīʿī textual heritage is in fact full of reports indicating that many companions were highly acclaimed. In fact, some contemporary Shīʿa scholars have written works on the companions whom the Shīʿa deem to be righteous and acceptable, and this list goes beyond 150 companions.[80] We invite the Imāmīyyah to dispel this stereotype and traditional conception of the Shīʿa that presents them as though they not only disagree with the companions but also accuse all of them of deviance and crime, excepting a handful. It is necessary to revisit this image to arrive at a much more nuanced stance not tarnished by ideology.

---

[79] This is a reference to a number of reports found in Shīʿī ḥadīth books that say every companion apostatized after the Prophet ﷺ due to their rejection of the divine authority of Imām ʿAlī except a handful of individuals.

[80] Unfortunately, many of these writings are untranslated and remain in Arabic. The Shīʿa scholar Sayyid Sharaf al-Dīn al-Mūsawī has written an article entitled الصحابة عند الشيعة الإمامية in which he enumerates these righteous companions exceeding over 150 names.

There are various Shīʿī traditions that indicate a very tolerant stance towards the companions in general, such as in the work written by Shaykh Ḥurr al-ʿĀmilī ﷺ (d. 1104 AH) in his treatise *Risālah fī Maʿrifah al-Ṣaḥābah* (A Memorandum on Recognition of the Companions). In this work he recounts the names of 481 companions and says:

"Know that most of the names that will be mentioned are devoid of any explicit attestation of reliability (*al-tawthīq*) and praise (*al-madḥ*), but if there is no condemnation (*al-dhamm*) narrated about them and there is nothing known about them that would warrant vilification (*al-qadḥ*), then their companionship itself is a type of praise."[81]

Shaykh al-Ḥurr al-ʿĀmilī ﷺ has put forth a principle here that the default for the companions of the Prophet ﷺ is their praiseworthiness unless known otherwise. It is not the case that the primary position regarding the companions of the Prophet ﷺ according to the Shīʿah is that they are all condemned unless known otherwise. Gathering all the Shīʿī reports and traditions that present a positive outlook of the

[81] al-Ḥurr al-ʿĀmilī, Shaykh Muḥammad b. al-Ḥasan, *Risālah fī Maʿrifat al-Ṣaḥābah*, p. 2.

companions can also assist in painting a much better picture of what was occurring in early Islamic history.[82]

Cursing of Revered Figures

Fourthly, perhaps what we have discussed so far on the topic of the companions is of trivial significance in the face of the topic of cursing the companions; a topic that is unfortunately an arena for bloodshed in Sunnī and Shīʿa relationships.

Although the famous and popular position of the Shīʿa scholars is that it is not obligatory to curse the companions, and in fact they do not allow cursing when it can result in harm for the Shīʿa themselves, the fact of the matter is – and I will be very blunt and clear on this – that the general Imāmī atmosphere is such that they do not prohibit nor see any problem with cursing some of the companions. In fact, cursing some of the companions is a habitual practice amongst a few of the

[82] Within the Shīʿa works, the respect for the companions is emphasized quite profusely and we will present a few of these narrations. In sermon 97 of *Nahj al-Balāghah*, Imām ʿAlī states: "I have seen the companions of the Prophet ﷺ, but I do not find anyone resembling them. They began the day with dust on the hair and face and passed the night in prostration and standing in prayers." Imām Zayn al-ʿĀbidīn, in his al-*Ṣaḥīfah al-Sajjādīyah*, has a whole supplication for blessing the companions of the Prophet ﷺ. Finally, Imām Jaʿfar al-Ṣādiq states as narrated in *al-Amālī* of Shaykh Ṭūsī: "I admonish you regarding the companions of your Prophet ﷺ: do not revile them."

Shīʿa and it is a practice that has intensified in recent times despite internal disputes and debates on this matter amongst the Shīʿa.

Regardless of theoretical and ijtihādī discussions, our message is one that rejects this practice and we do not consider it to be a desirable practice as far as a healthy religious culture is concerned. With full audacity, we invite the Shīʿī Imāmī Marjaʿīyyah to maintain a clear and bold position against this malicious practice which continues to deteriorate and slip out of control. We believe that slandering the revered figures of other Muslims and harming their sentiments is not a justified practice – will any Imāmī accept and tolerate the cursing of any one of the Ahl al-Bayt ﷺ? If any person were to do such a thing, the Shīʿa themselves will consider them to be disbelievers and give the religious verdict of execution for blaspheming against the Ahl al-Bayt ﷺ. So why do we not respect the sentiments of the rest of the Muslims today by not slandering their revered figures, just as we expect and demand respect of our revered figures?

Furthermore, why do we not expect them to react when we permit ourselves to curse their revered figures publicly, completely inattentive to their sentiments and rights upon us as Muslims; but if they were to say anything about our revered figures, we will be ready to issue statements on their disbelief and execution for blasphemy?!

Our message is that we need to do away with this habit that is prevalent amongst some Shīʿa, as well as do away with the logic of excommunicating one another. If there does need to be an approach to dealing with this matter, then it needs to be done through conveying one's opinion with transparency regarding what the Shīʿa perspective is about the historical events that transpired in the first Islamic generations. This is a much better approach and in line with a ḥadīth from Imām ʿAlī ﷺ where he has been reported to have said: "I dislike that you be known as cursers and abusers."[83]

We announce our absolute rejection of attempts at censorship regarding the companions while also rejecting excommunication of anyone who has an opposing opinion to the Ahl al-Sunnah on the matter of the trustworthiness of the companions. Likewise, we reject the phenomenon of cursing, swearing, and slandering the revered figures of other Muslims, like some of the companions and mothers of the believers. In addition, we reject all other disgraceful behavior that is committed in this same vein, like the events that take

---

[83] al-Mīrzā al-Nūrī, *Mustadrak al-Wasāʾil*, Vol. 12, p. 306.

place on the 9th of Rabīʿ al-Awwal in some minority Imāmī communities.[84]

We demand that such disgraceful discourse be changed to a more academic one, one where each group among us can freely—yet ethically and calmly—express their views regarding what transpired in history.

I do not know why there is so much insistence in silencing critics of some of the companions while these are legitimate historiographical matters and are subject to criticism only within an academic context. If we are convinced in the strength of our opinion regarding the trustworthiness of all companions (*ʿadālah al-ṣaḥābah*), then let others critique this principle and let us respond to its premises with the strength of logic, knowledge, and evidence - not with excommunication, intimidation, criminalization, and repression!

Has censorship about the companions by the Ahl al-Sunnah ever result in any productive result after more

[84] This is a reference to the Eid al-Zahrā celebration, in which a minority of Shīʿa celebrate the demise of the Second Caliph ʿUmar b. al-Khaṭṭāb. It is notable that there is no convincing historical evidence regarding this being the date of his death. Anyone who is even a little familiar with Shīʿa-Sunnī polemics will realize that these practices have fueled tensions and lead to animosity. For more information, please refer to the article on Iqra Online entitled, "*Celebrating 9th Rabīʿ al-Awwal—What For?*"

than a thousand years? Indeed, it has not resulted in anything except further turmoil and challenges, the downfall of some Islamic governing systems, and further provocative insistence by the companions' detractors.

I also do not know why there is so much insistence in the practice of verbal cursing (*al-la'n*), given it is not obligatory and it is not considered from the primary tenets of belief of the Shī'a. Is the shedding of Muslim blood today such a trivial matter that we are willing to allow it and be content with it, while at the same time deeming cursing and denigration such a vital affair that we must remain insistent on it – even though it is not obligatory as per the verdict of the greatest of Imāmī jurisconsults (*kibār al-marāji'*)?[85]

Why do such people not investigate and see whether even one of the greatest Imāmī jurisconsult obligates such cursing and denigration? Is this an obligatory religious duty? Does it not behoove one to abandon this recommended act – if it is even proven to be recommended – for the sake of the protection of

[85] To the contrary, in fact many Shī'a authorities today have in fact prohibited the cursing of the revered figures of Ahl al-Sunnah including Āyatullāh Khāmina'ī, Āyatullāh Sīstānī, and Āyatullāh Nāṣir Makārim Shīrāzī. For more information regarding this, please refer to the book "*Mutual Respect and Peaceful Co-existence Among Muslims,*" compiled by Sayyid Muḥammad Rizvi.

Muslim blood and to safeguard the unity and dignity of the ever-so-fragile remains of our Muslim community?

Was it not the Umayyad dynasty that initiated the practice of swearing, slandering, and cursing in Islamic history – as many scholars acknowledge – by cursing ʿAlī and his progeny on the pulpits for decades?! It is not appropriate for the vociferous detractors of the Umayyad dynasty to imitate them, rather they should instead adopt the moral high ground by insisting on maintaining an ethical demeanor while still being critical of history and highlighting the shortcomings that occurred.

Is it desirable that the Muslim community today – instead of reviving itself – remains fighting with one another over historical matters in a way that it ends in the cursing, swearing, and suppression of huge swathes of people? Is it expected that we remain happy and delighted with such practices while we see the Islamic community falling behind on many fronts due to these fights? Should it not instead be the expectation that we take this matter very seriously and instead give reform and rectification of the Muslims' situation utmost priority?

The Mothers of the Believers (*ummahāt al-mu'minīn*): Between Purity and Reverence

Fifthly, in this context the discussion arises regarding the stance on the Mothers of the Believers, especially 'Ā'isha who is described as the mother of believers whether we like it or not. Accusing her or any of the other wives with obscenities and slandering them is simply a rejected and condemned act, let alone publishing such opinions in the public sphere!

Some Imāmī Shī'a scholars have referred to the wives of the Prophet ﷺ as "The Mothers of Reverence." 'Allāmah Muḥammad Baḥr al-'Ulūm ؒ (d. 1326 AH) has said: "Know that the word mother has three meanings: biological mothers, mothers of milk kinship, and mothers of reverence and magnificence – and the wives of the Prophet ﷺ are from the third category as they are the mothers of the believers...".[86]

The honor of the Prophet ﷺ is our honor, and the Shī'a consider all Prophets ؑ to be free from any detested quality and upon this principle some scholars have mentioned that a wife of a Prophet ؑ cannot commit adultery because that is one of those detested qualities. It is for this reason that the betrayal of some of the wives of the Prophets ؑ as mentioned in the Qur'ān is seen as

[86] al-'Ulūm, 'Allāmah Muḥammad Baḥr, *Bulgha al-Faqīh*, Vol. 3, p. 206-207.

referring to non-licentious betrayal. One can refer to the works of exegesis for more information.[87]

Calling Shīʿa Religious Authorities Towards Bold Historical Stances

We therefore implore the religious figures who are sources of recourse for people to follow the footsteps of the religious jurisconsults such as Āyatullāh Sayyid ʿAlī Sīstānī, Āyatullāh Sayyid ʿAlī Khāminaʾī, Āyatullāh Sayyid Muḥammad Ḥusayn Faḍlullāh ﵀, Āyatullāh Sayyid Maḥmūd Hāshimī Shāhrūdī ﵀ and Āyatullāh Muḥammad Āṣif Muḥsinī ﵀, who have all issued statements and religious verdicts clarifying their positions against the practice of cursing the companions or slandering any one of the wives of the Prophet ﷺ. We implore religious figures to not suffice with just silence on this matter, even if they are already in agreement with the statements of the aforementioned scholars.

Notwithstanding, is the solution to this problem really violence, killing, and butchering of the Shīʿa wherever they are found? Will taking such steps and passing fatwas of excommunication and attacking the Shīʿa really end the transgression by some on the honor of the Prophet ﷺ? Will not this retaliatory violence instead compound and increase the magnitude of these

[87] For example, see al-Tabrīsī, *Jawāmiʿ al-Jāmiʿ*, Vol. 3, p. 596.

transgressions? Is it not better that we put an end to the source of radicalism by having the moderates from both camps meet in the middle and implement a strategic roadmap to deal with such radicalism?

Calling the Sunnī Religious Authorities Towards Taking a Bold Stance in Reference to the Prophetic Ahl al-Bayt ﷺ

Sixthly, we have various observations and criticisms on certain positions taken by many of the Ahl al-Sunnah. We find it necessary for them to also reconsider their approach for the sake of Muslim unity, in line with the practice of the Prophet ﷺ who has commanded us to do so as found in numerous traditions present in the books of both groups. What I am referring to is the widespread acknowledgement of the status of the Imāms of the Ahl al-Bayt ﷺ—as considered by the Shīʿa—in the consciousness of the Sunnī psyche.

Why is one of the greatest tragedies which befell the grandson of the Prophet ﷺ along with his family and companions in Karbalāʾ, kept hidden? Why is there a forgetful and indifferent attitude taken towards this event and even at times attempts to obfuscate it? If our slogan is indeed the love of the family and companions of the Prophet ﷺ, then we must be loyal to it so that our bonds of friendship can increase around it while allowing a greater opportunity for connection between us Muslims.

We therefore summon towards reviving the remembrance of the Ahl al-Bayt 🕮 and the Imāms of the Shīʿa, whom all of the Ahl al-Sunnah respect and revere. We also call towards maintaining a clear and unwavering stance against all those who oppressed the Ahl al-Bayt 🕮 throughout the course of history, especially in the Umayyad and ʿAbbāsid eras. We ought to be fair with the Prophetic household by condemning Yazīd b. Muʿāwiyah and his allies instead of critiquing the stance of Imām al-Ḥusayn 🕮 by saying he revolted against the leader of his time!

Does anyone despise and hate Imām Jaʿfar al-Ṣādiq 🕮 or have enmity with Imām Zayn al-ʿĀbidīn Sayyid al-Sājidīn 🕮, or do all Muslims categorically feel proud of them and the family of the Prophet 🕮 in general? Aren't the traditions in praise of the Ahl al-Bayt 🕮 in the books of all Muslims innumerable? Do there not exist an abundance of reports in the books of the Ahl al-Sunnah that speak of the Umayyad and ʿAbbāsid caliphate in a negative way while this is plastered over in the general culture amongst the Sunnīs and it is generally purported that Umayyad history was glorious or that its good was greater than its evil by a great margin?!

If a Sunnī has an issue with an Imāmī who follows the Ahl al-Bayt 🕮, this also does not mean that one extends this issue to the Ahl al-Bayt 🕮 themselves – as if one will take revenge against those who they have an issue with by taking revenge against figures who are revered by all of us. As God ﷻ has said in the Qur'ān:

﴿قُلْ أَغَيْرَ اللَّهِ أَبْغِي رَبًّا وَهُوَ رَبُّ كُلِّ شَيْءٍ ۚ وَلَا تَكْسِبُ كُلُّ نَفْسٍ إِلَّا عَلَيْهَا ۚ وَلَا تَزِرُ وَازِرَةٌ وِزْرَ أُخْرَىٰ ۚ ثُمَّ إِلَىٰ رَبِّكُمْ مَرْجِعُكُمْ فَيُنَبِّئُكُمْ بِمَا كُنْتُمْ فِيهِ تَخْتَلِفُونَ﴾

qul 'a-ghayra llāhi 'abghī rabban wa-huwa rabbu kulli shay'in wa-lā taksibu kullu nafsin 'illā 'alayhā wa-lā taziru wāziratun wizra 'ukhrā thumma 'ilā rabbikum marji'ukum fa-yunabbi'ukum bi-mā kuntum fīhi takhtalifūn ᵃ﴿

﴿*Say, 'Shall I seek a Lord other than God, while He is the Lord of all things?' No soul does evil except against itself, and no bearer shall bear another's burden; then to your Lord will be your return, whereat He will inform you concerning that about which you used to differ.*﴾[88]

﴿مَنِ اهْتَدَىٰ فَإِنَّمَا يَهْتَدِي لِنَفْسِهِ ۖ وَمَنْ ضَلَّ فَإِنَّمَا يَضِلُّ عَلَيْهَا ۚ وَلَا تَزِرُ وَازِرَةٌ وِزْرَ أُخْرَىٰ ۗ وَمَا كُنَّا مُعَذِّبِينَ حَتَّىٰ نَبْعَثَ رَسُولًا﴾

---

[88] Sūrat al-Anʿām, Verse 164.

*ʾmani htadā fa-'innamā yahtadī li-nafsihī wa-man ḍalla
fa-'innamā yaḍillu ʿalayhā wa-lā taziru wāziratun wizra
'ukhrā wa-mā kunnā muʿadhdhibīna ḥattā nabʿatha
rasūla ⁿ*

*Whoever is guided is guided only for [the good of] his own
soul, and whoever goes astray, goes astray only to its
detriment. No bearer shall bear another's burden. We do not
punish [any community] until We have sent [it] an
apostle.*[89]

What we are advocating is that the educational/cultural
ministries and the religious institutions of the Islamic
world take serious directed steps towards reviving
awareness of the personalities of Ahl al-Bayt, who
were among the most knowledgeable ones with regards
to revelation and that which was revealed upon the
Prophet and were also amongst the most scholastic in
understanding the Qurʾān and Sunnah.

We hope that this may allow for the laity among Ahl al-
Sunnah to become familiar with the Ahl al-Bayt and
their teachings while fomenting more remembrance of
the circumstances and events that occurred during their
lives. Indeed, we should ask why works like *Nahj al-
Balāghah*, *al-Ṣaḥīfa al-Sajjādīyyah*, or the *Risālah al-
Ḥuqūq* and other valuable works of the Ahl al-Bayt

---

[89] Sūrat al-Isrāʾ, Verse 15.

should be rendered absent from the life of a Sunnī Muslim?! Likewise, we hope that the Imāmī Shīʿa would become more familiar with the accomplishments of the companions and the successive generations (*tābiʿīn*), especially those whom they see no issue with. Why is the history of the conquests, in which many companions participated, kept hidden under the auspices of insistence in rejecting any positive quality that the companions possessed?

If you have an issue with a certain companion, this does not mean that you eradicate and dismiss even their good qualities, or that you become indifferent towards all the noble companions. How could we presume this while we see that the Qurʾān goes as far as to praise the disbelievers in some of their qualities despite their disbelief, and the Sunnah of the Prophet ﷺ also attests to this?

The Logic of the Qurʾān in Calling for Justice and Equality

In this vein, let us also reflect on these verses of the Qurʾān that demonstrate God's ﷻ praise of those who are not even Muslims:

﴿وَمِنْ أَهْلِ الْكِتَابِ مَنْ إِنْ تَأْمَنْهُ بِقِنْطَارٍ يُؤَدِّهِ إِلَيْكَ وَمِنْهُمْ مَنْ إِنْ تَأْمَنْهُ بِدِينَارٍ لَا يُؤَدِّهِ إِلَيْكَ إِلَّا مَا دُمْتَ عَلَيْهِ قَائِمًا ۗ ذَٰلِكَ بِأَنَّهُمْ قَالُوا لَيْسَ عَلَيْنَا فِي الْأُمِّيِّينَ سَبِيلٌ وَيَقُولُونَ عَلَى اللَّهِ الْكَذِبَ وَهُمْ يَعْلَمُونَ﴾

﴿wa-min ʾahli l-kitābi man ʾin taʾmanhu bi-qinṭārin yuʾaddihī ʾilayka wa-minhum man ʾin taʾmanhu bi-dīnārin lā yuʾaddihī ʾilayka ʾillā mā dumta ʿalayhi qāʾiman dhālika bi-ʾannahum qālū laysa ʿalaynā fī l-ʾummiyyīna sabīlun wa-yaqūlūna ʿalā llāhi l-kadhiba wa-hum yaʿlamūn [a]﴾

﴿And among the People of the Book is he who if you entrust him with a quintal will repay it to you, and among them is he who, if you entrust him with a dinar will not repay it to you unless you stand persistently over him. That is because they say, 'We have no obligation to the non-Jews.' But they attribute lies to God, and they know [it].*[90]﴾

Though some people from the Ahl al-Kitāb do not return back the trusts, this did not prevent the Qur'ān

[90] Sūrat Āl ʿImrān, Verse 75.

* Quintal: hundredweight. *The American Heritage Dictionary* gives the following history of the English 'quintal': Middle English, a unit of weight, from Old French, from Medieval Latin *quintāle*, from Arabic *qinṭār*, from Late Greek *kentēnarion*, from Late Latin *centēnārium* (pondus), hundred(weight), from Latin *centēnārius*, of a hundred.

from being fair and just in mentioning those from the Ahl al-Kitāb who do return back their trusts. This is the culture that the Qur'ān is creating and alluding towards: a culture of justice and fairness.

﴿لَتَجِدَنَّ أَشَدَّ النَّاسِ عَدَاوَةً لِّلَّذِينَ آمَنُوا الْيَهُودَ وَالَّذِينَ أَشْرَكُوا ۖ وَلَتَجِدَنَّ أَقْرَبَهُم مَّوَدَّةً لِّلَّذِينَ آمَنُوا الَّذِينَ قَالُوا إِنَّا نَصَارَىٰ ۚ ذَٰلِكَ بِأَنَّ مِنْهُمْ قِسِّيسِينَ وَرُهْبَانًا وَأَنَّهُمْ لَا يَسْتَكْبِرُونَ﴾

﴿la-tajidanna 'ashadda n-nāsi 'adāwatan li-lladhīna 'āmanū l-yahūda wa-lladhīna 'ashrakū wa-la-tajidanna 'aqrabahum mawaddatan li-lladhīna 'āmanū lladhīna qālū 'innā naṣārā dhālika bi-'anna minhum qissīsīna wa-ruhbānan wa-'annahum lā yastakbirūn [a]﴾

﴿*Surely* You *will find the most hostile of all people towards the faithful to be the Jews and the polytheists, and surely you will find the nearest of them in affection to the faithful to be those who say 'We are Christians.' That is because there are priests and monks among them, and because they are not arrogant.*﴾[91]

The Qur'ān teaches us that our enmity with some groups of people or individuals should not push us to behave with them unjustly and unfairly.

---

[91] Sūrat al-Mā'idah, Verse 82.

Likewise, God ﷻ says in the Qurʾān:

﴿يَا أَيُّهَا الَّذِينَ آمَنُوا لَا تُحِلُّوا شَعَائِرَ اللَّهِ وَلَا الشَّهْرَ الْحَرَامَ وَلَا الْهَدْيَ
وَلَا الْقَلَائِدَ وَلَا آمِّينَ الْبَيْتَ الْحَرَامَ يَبْتَغُونَ فَضْلًا مِنْ رَبِّهِمْ وَرِضْوَانًا ۚ
وَإِذَا حَلَلْتُمْ فَاصْطَادُوا ۚ وَلَا يَجْرِمَنَّكُمْ شَنَآنُ قَوْمٍ أَنْ صَدُّوكُمْ عَنِ
الْمَسْجِدِ الْحَرَامِ أَنْ تَعْتَدُوا ۘ وَتَعَاوَنُوا عَلَى الْبِرِّ وَالتَّقْوَىٰ ۖ وَلَا تَعَاوَنُوا
عَلَى الْإِثْمِ وَالْعُدْوَانِ ۚ وَاتَّقُوا اللَّهَ ۖ إِنَّ اللَّهَ شَدِيدُ الْعِقَابِ﴾

﴿*yā-ʾayyuhā lladhīna ʾāmanū lā tuḥillū shaʿāʾira llāhi wa-lā sh-shahra l-ḥarāma wa-lā l-hadya wa-lā l-qalāʾida wa-lā ʾāmmīna l-bayta l-ḥarāma yabtaghūna faḍlan min rabbihim wa-riḍwānan wa-ʾidhā ḥalaltum fa-ṣṭādū wa-lā yajrimannakum shanaʾānu qawmin ʾan ṣaddūkum ʿani l-masjidi l-ḥarāmi ʾan taʿtadū wa-taʿāwanū ʿalā l-birri wa-t-taqwā wa-lā taʿāwanū ʿalā l-ʾithmi wa-l-ʿudwāni wa-ttaqū llāha ʾinna llāha shadīdu l-ʿiqāb*[1]﴾

﴿*O you who have faith! Do not violate God's sacraments, neither the sacred month*, nor the offering*, nor the necklaces, nor those bound* for the Sacred House who seek their Lord's grace and [His] pleasure. But when you emerge from pilgrim sanctity you may hunt for game. Ill feeling for a people should not lead you, because they barred you from [entering] the Sacred Mosque, to transgress.*

Cooperate in piety and Godwariness, but do not cooperate in sin and aggression, and be wary of God. Indeed God is severe in retribution.﴿[92]

﴿يَا أَيُّهَا الَّذِينَ آمَنُوا كُونُوا قَوَّامِينَ لِلَّهِ شُهَدَاءَ بِالْقِسْطِ ۖ وَلَا يَجْرِمَنَّكُمْ شَنَآنُ قَوْمٍ عَلَىٰ أَلَّا تَعْدِلُوا ۚ اعْدِلُوا هُوَ أَقْرَبُ لِلتَّقْوَىٰ ۖ وَاتَّقُوا اللَّهَ ۚ إِنَّ اللَّهَ خَبِيرٌ بِمَا تَعْمَلُونَ﴾

﴾*yā-'ayyuhā lladhīna 'āmanū kūnū qawwāmīna li-llāhi shuhadā'a bi-l-qisṭi wa-lā yajrimannakum shana'ānu qawmin ʿalā 'allā taʿdilū ʿdilū huwa 'aqrabu li-t-taqwā wa-ttaqū llāha 'inna llāha khabīrun bi-mā taʿmalūn* [a]﴿

﴾*O you who have faith! Be maintainers, as witnesses for the sake of God, of justice*, and ill feeling for a people should never lead you to be unfair.*

---

[92] Surah al-Mā'idah, Verse 2.

* That is, the month of Dhū al-Ḥijjah, during which the *ḥajj* is performed.

* That is, the sheep, camel or cow brought for the sacrifice. The 'necklaces' mean the token objects hung around the neck of the sacrificial animal.

* That is, the pilgrims heading for *ḥajj* or *ʿumrah*.

Be fair; that is nearer to Godwariness, and be wary of God. God is indeed well aware of what you do.﴿[93]

We say all of this because we believe that the truth has a right to be uttered and followed. As such, we can get closer to one another and understand the history of our revered figures while increasing our respect for Islam and its deeply rooted traditions.

Ending on this same point, we also want to point the attention of both groups – the Sunnīs and the Imāmīyyah – towards rejuvenating the remembrance of Zayd b. ʿAlī b. al-Ḥusayn b. ʿAlī b. Abī Ṭālib: particularly his feats, piety, and religiosity. Indeed, he is one of the symbols of the Ahl al-Bayt عليهم السلام who are respected by all Muslims today as far as we know.

Distortion (*al-taḥrīf*) of the Noble Qurʾān and Denial of the Prophetic Tradition

The issue of distortion of the Qurʾān has not ceased to be a point of contention among some Muslims with the Shīʿa Imāmis being accused of adopting the view that the Qurʾān has been distorted. Although this calumny has gradually seen a decline in the past few decades

[93] Surah al-Māʾidah, Verse 8.

* Confer. 4:135.

thanks to many of the Ahl al-Sunnah paying it more close attention, there still remain some religious currents that insist on propagating these controversial claims.

We would like to admit here that in some of the Imāmī ḥadīth collections there are some narrations from which distortion in the Qur'ān may be gleaned; and we also fully recognize that a minority of Shī'a Imāmī scholars in our history have adopted this position. However, does this mean that the Shī'a as a whole, especially today, believe in the distortion of the Qur'ān?!

Our invitation to our brothers from Ahl al-Sunnah on this point is to think contextually about this sensitive issue and to have awareness about the nature of how the Shī'a form their religious convictions. Even if the Shī'a ḥadīth sources do imply distortion of the Qur'ān (although many Shī'a scholars have their own perspectives and interpretations that render it far-fetched), this does not necessarily imply that the Shī'a believe in the distortion of the Qur'ān. The Shī'a assimilate their religious beliefs through reference to the contemporary authorities on the issue and not directly from their ancient literature. The door of intellectual struggle in ascertaining the truth (*al-ijtihād*) is still deemed open among them and it is well-recognized that they do not allow emulation (*al-taqlīd*) of deceased scholars. As a result, the fundamental convictions of the Shī'a are not derived except through this well-established connection between the laity and their contemporary scholars.

In turn, this implies that in order for me to understand the fundamental Imāmī beliefs of today, it is necessary for me to reference their scholarly institutions and contemporary religious authorities; it is completely inappropriate to reference such-and-such scholars that lived over one thousand years ago or narrations from their old books given that the Shīʿa Imāmīs themselves do not refer to such sources and that they typically obtain their views instead from the intellectual struggles wrought out by latter-day and contemporary scholars and authorities.

Therefore, even if it is uncovered in the course of Islamic history that certain personalities endorsed the view of distortion of the Qurʾān, it still stands to reason that the majority of Imāmīs—especially the latter-day intellectual giants among them—hold an almost unanimous consensus upon the belief of the Qurʾān's immaculate preservation against all distortion, interpolation, or redaction.[94] Therefore, what is the need to aggrandize this issue and grant it such an exaggerated importance? When have the Shīʿa ever kept another Qurʾān other than the popularized one within their homes?[95]

Furthermore, where are the manuscripts that substantiate the existence of another Qurʾān among the Shīʿa? To the contrary, their reciters, memorizers, and commentators (dozens of Qurʾānic commentaries exist among the Shīʿa) substantiate that there is no other

[94] Endorsement of *taḥrīf* in the Qurʾān was famously made by al-Mīrzā Ḥusayn al-Muḥaddith al-Nūrī (d. 1320 AH), although it was immediately and thoroughly refuted by Shīʿa scholars, even within his lifetime. A detailed exposition of the issue of taḥrīf and analysis of the Shīʿī narrations about it can be found in Āyatullāh Sayyid Abū al-Qāsim Mūsawī Khūʾī work "*The Prolegomena to the Qurʾān* (*al-Bayān fī Tafsīr al-Qurʾān*)" translated by ʿAbdulazīz Sachedina.

[95] This is a reference to another commonly held misconception that the Shīʿa have an alternative Qurʾān named "*Muṣḥaf Fāṭimah,*" which is clearly a great slander. Other claims that are made are that the Shīʿa add two fabricated sūrahs named *al-Wilāyah* and *al-Nurayn* in their Qurʾān, which is also another blatantly false accusation.

book that they alternatively view as the Qurʾān.[96] Even further, the Qurʾān they have in their homes is itself most often the one published under the authority of Saudi Arabia; therefore, why is there all this commotion? What is the purpose of all this excessive media coverage on the topic? Is it justified that each time somebody claims something it is necessary that we stereotype the entire sect and blow it up to make it a large issue?

It is about time that we move past this issue especially given the various Shīʿī achievements—especially over the past century—in the realm of commentary on the Qurʾān, memorization, and in its teaching and specialization.[97] Before us lie the various Shīʿa universities and institutions that assign various specializations in Qurʾānic studies as well as the Shīʿa

---

[96] There are some 30 Shīʿa commentary works on the Qurʾān available in Arabic, although four are particularly well-known: *Tafsīr al-Ṣāfī* by Mullā Muḥammad b. Murtaḍā Fayḍ Kāshānī ﵀ (d. 1091 AH), *Tafsīr al-Tibyān* by Shaykh Muḥammad b. Ḥasan Ṭūsī ﵀ (d. 460 AH), *Tafsīr Majmaʿ al-Bayān* by Shaykh Abū ʿAlī Ṭabarsī ﵀ (d. 468 AH), and *Tafsīr al-Mīzān* by ʿAllāmah Sayyid Muḥammad Ḥusayn Ṭabāṭabāʾī ﵀ (d. 1402). Of course, in Persian, Turkish, and Urdu languages the number of Shīʿah tafāsīr easily exceeds over one hundred.

[97] Since the Islāmic revolution in Irān, there has been a widespread growth in Shīʿa representation in the Qurʾānic sciences. For example, Iran holds an annual international Qurʾān competition for Muslims from all over the world.

scholars who have published thousands of books related to the Qur'ān.[98] Is it indeed not time that after all this emphasis from the Shīʿa on the preservation of the Qur'ān that we remove this notion from circulation? Are there indeed not also narrations among the books of the Ahl al-Sunnah that also point towards distortion (*al-taḥrīf*)? Is it acceptable to launch calumny based on this same premise?![99]

The other issue here is the claim that the Shīʿa reject the tradition of the Prophet ﷺ and only accept the tradition of the Ahl al-Bayt عليهم السلام. I believe it behooves those who are endowed with intellect and expertise to deepen their analysis on this topic and brush off its concomitant historical fallacies.

Indubitably, among the Shīʿa ḥadīth collections—and this is a solemn statement wrought out by extensive research—there are thousands of Prophetic narrations.

---

[98] The number of books that the Shīʿa have produced about the Qur'ān and related sciences of theology (*al-kalām*), jurisprudence (*al-fiqh*), Arabic language (*al-lughah*), commentary (*al-tafsīr*), and Qur'ānic sciences (*ʿulūm al-Qur'ān*) indeed number in the tens of thousands. A famous Shīʿa encyclopedic index written by Āghā Buzurg al-Tihrānī entitled "*al-Dharīʿah ilā Taṣānīf al-Shīʿa*" (*The Path to Shīʿa Manuscripts*)" lists over 50,000 Shīʿa works by name and author in 25 volumes.

[99] Among these Sunnī ḥadīth is the one narrated by ʿĀ'isha in *Sunan b. Mājah*, Hadīth n. 2020 which alleges that there was a verse of stoning and suckling in the Qur'ān that were eaten by a goat.

Therefore, on what grounds can it be claimed that the Shī'a have abandoned the Prophetic tradition?!

Does the Imāmī Stance in Not Accepting the Impeccability of the Ṣaḥābah Really Destroy the Prophetic Sunnah?

The issue here is that some of us presume lack of belief in the absolute trustworthiness of the Companions (*'adālah al-ṣaḥābah*) necessitates cutting the tie of connection between us and the Prophetic era. This is predicated upon the belief that the Companions are the first generation that transmitted to us the events of that time; thus, if we claim that they are not trustworthy, then this entire intermediary is rendered void and we cannot rely on any information regarding that period. Hence, we are faced with obstruction of all access to the Prophetic tradition. However, the truth is that this is not the case; for even if the Imāmīs do not accept the absolute trustworthiness of all the Companions, there remains for them two ways to substantiate the Prophetic tradition:

1. The companions which they deem reliable; this is because although the Imāmīs reject the theory of absolute trustworthiness of all Companions, they do not hold a negative stance in reference to all companions and reject all their narrations (may refuge be with God ﷻ for such a claim). Instead, the

majority of Shīʿa scholars have a negative stance only in reference to a limited number of them while deeming the majority of companions acceptable such as Jābir b. ʿAbd Allah al-Anṣārī, Abū Saʿīd al-Khudrī, ʿAbdullāh b. Masʿūd, ʿAmmār b. Yāsir, Umm Salamah, Asmāʾ b. ʿUmays, Ḥudhayfah b. al-Yamān, Khuzaymah b. Thābit, ʿAbdullāh b. ʿAbbās, Abū Dharr al-Ghifārī, al-Miqdād b. al-Aswad al-Kindī, Hujr b. ʿAdī, Abu Ayyūb al-Anṣārī, Khabbāb b. al-Aratt, Qays b. Saʿd b. ʿUbādah, Ubayy b. Kaʿb, Salmān al-Fārisī al-Muḥammadī, etc. Therefore, it is a massive fallacy to presume that there is no acceptable companion to the Shīʿa.

2. The Ahl al-Bayt 🕮; who are themselves scholars of the Prophetic tradition and narrate his hadith from one generation to the next as they themselves state unambiguously in the Shīʿa narrations. It was on this basis that massive encyclopedias were compiled that expound on the laws of the Sharīʿa and it was on this basis that their transmission was preserved generation after generation through the proverbial golden chain (*al-Silsilah al-Dhahabiyyah*) going back to the Prophet 🕮.

Based on the above, I think it is important for us to also remove these claims from circulation in order that there not be any imaginary barrier that limits our mutual corroboration and communication. Indeed, the Shīʿa do not deem the tradition of the Ahl al-Bayt 🕮 to be anything other than the self-same tradition of the Prophet ﷺ. Rather, they regard what the Ahl al-Bayt ؑ say to be derived directly from their forefathers on the authority of Imām ʿAlī, Sayyidah Fāṭimah, Imām Ḥasan, and Imām Ḥusayn ؑ who in turn narrate on the authority of the Prophet ﷺ. They are not lawgivers as per the majority of the Shīʿa scholars (although there is a minority that disagrees); rather they convey to us with pristine accuracy the commandments and concepts that the Prophet ﷺ had taught. By no means are they deemed a substitute for the Prophet ﷺ or the role of the Noble Qurʾān.

Towards Establishing General Islamic Ḥadīth Databases

We therefore issue a call to our brethren from other denominations: let us come together to establish relations with one another and extinguish the misconceptions that we have conjured up about one another. Even more, our call is also that the Imāmīs should endeavor to benefit to some extent from the ḥadīth of Ahl al-Sunnah while the Ahl al-Sunnah should attempt to benefit to some extent from the hadith of the Shīʿa. It is no longer acceptable to continue this schism between us regarding what we have inherited of our literature on the authority of the Prophet ﷺ. Our conviction wrought out by investigation is that the authenticated Prophetic hadith are present and distributed within the collections of all

Islamic denominations and that we must develop a well-grounded methodology to extract and uncover them.

Our invitation is namely this: that we establish contemporary non-denominational Islamic databases (subsuming other denominations such as the Ibāḍīs and the Zaydīs) that make available the largest number of Prophetic hadith possible to the disposal of the researcher who is then free to select which hadith meet the criteria of authentication based on analysis of the chain (*al-sanad*) and content (*al-matn*); creating this in addition to an encyclopedia for rijāli studies in accordance with all sects would play a crucial role in establishing better epistemological relations between various Muslim sects.

Dissimulation (*al-Taqiyyah*) and the Crisis of Confidence

Dissimulation in the view of the Imāmīs is a method of preserving the Shīʿa community in the face of reigning authorities that enact oppression against them. The Imāms of the Ahl al-Bayt ﷺ have allowed an individual to pray or practice his religious duties in a non-Shīʿa jurisprudential manner if revealing their identity (either through action or speech) would result in harm or sour relations with other denominations. In fact, this understanding of dissimulation is accepted by many Muslim scholars with only minor variances. Rather, when we examine the issue more closely, we see that dissimulation has long been practiced by suppressed minorities in difficult circumstances; even those who do not have any religious inclination have been observed to practice it.

Nonetheless, in the view of many among Ahl al-Sunnah dissimulation is regarded as one of the most undermining barriers towards the establishment of trustworthiness between the Sunnīs and Shīʿas. They state that they cannot trust a Shīʿa individual because everything that he utters is not honest due to the use of dissimulation—he states that which he himself does not believe. They note that when the practice of dissimulation spreads in society, it is natural that it will destroy all forms of mutual collaboration. The Shīʿa begin to create a secret belief system which they do not reveal: a hypocritical sect with whom it is not possible to have genuine relations, safety, or trust. Hence, they declare that the Shīʿa are in fact disbelievers clothing themselves in Islamic garb disguised by the practice of dissimulation.

There are those who continue to propagate this conception and work tirelessly to establish it in the public Islamic consciousness; as a result, a great breach of trust is fomented between the Imāmī Shīʿas and other sects through which it is rendered impossible to establish a harmonious Islamic society based on well-grounded relationships.

As we have stated in this memorandum, we aim towards brevity and do not want to belabor or treat these issues exhaustively. Let us take it for granted that the phenomenon of dissimulation exists among the Imāmīs and assume full cognizance about its presence; the pertinent questions are then as follows:

Why Did the Practice of Dissimulation Emerge?

As for this first question, I believe that the policy of suppression, terrorism, tyranny, and castration practiced by a great number of Muslim statesmen, over the course of history and to the present-day, has played a prominent role in the fomenting of dissimulation as a particular mode of lifestyle among the Imāmīs and others. What do you want a suppressed minority—stripped of its rights of freedom of expression and opinion—to do? If they were to say that "we do not believe in the absolute trustworthiness of the companions," they would be accused of disbelief or innovation and possibly imprisoned, murdered, or pillaged. If any other faction would be in their situation living in such a manner for centuries, wouldn't dissimulation become a part of their religious culture?! Should such a faction be deemed the criminal or should the culprit instead be those oppressive governments that never acknowledged freedom of expression, belief, or opinion and actively suppressed the rights of divergence, critique, and debate?! Add to this the fact that a great number of Muslim scholars also supported them by issuing fatwas that legalized murder and excommunication of the Shīʿa? This is the most prominent historical reason for the emergence of this phenomenon, although it is certainly not the only one.[100]

I am not implying by the above that Shīʿa statesmen over the course of history have been just. I certainly do not espouse belief in the infallibility of sects or their histories—in fact I believe that the crux of reformation in the Muslim community resides in liberating ourselves from this notion of sects being infallible. However, the situation is dramatically different because there is nothing in the Sunnī belief system or practice that is deemed contentious to Shīʿa statesmen such that they would oppress them in the name of religion. The Sunnī lack of belief for instance in the doctrine of Imāmah is tolerable to the Shīʿa and the latter would deem it a mere difference of opinion. On the contrary, the very title of "Shīʿa" engenders controversy in the general Sunnī

---

[100] The oppression of the Shīʿa extended from the beginning of the reign of the Umayyads until the present-day amidst groups like the extremist Islamic State and Wahhābī movements that call for the excommunication and execution of the Shīʿa, deeming their beliefs blasphemous. The site www.shiarightswatch.org carries contemporary news about Shīʿa persecution around the world.

populace and even complete repudiation, given their perceived stance about the Ṣaḥābah.

All this implies that the conception of dissimulation will only dissipate with the rendering of intellectual freedom to minorities and with the Shīʿa themselves also rising up to assimilate further into the general society. If this should be possible, it would only be a tincture of time for these mistaken perceptions to change.

Has Dissimulation Continued to Be a Barrier to Understanding the Shīʿa?

As for this second question, we believe that in the current age the question of the secret face of the Shīʿa is no longer relevant. Indeed, the books of the Shīʿa, their intellectual and political stances, their internal conflicts, and even their gathering places and ḥusayniyyahs are completely exposed to public view. In the wake of the information explosion era and social media, there is nothing else that remains to be discovered. I believe that anyone who wants to witness the Shīʿa atmosphere today is able to now do that with every facility, even if it had been difficult in the past.

Rather, I would firmly point out that if the practices of the Imāmīs were based on dissimulation, then how was it that for centuries the Ahl al-Sunnah were able to know of the phenomenon of cursing and the stance of the Imāmīs regarding the caliphs and the companions?!

This clearly implies that their books had been publicly available and that it was possible to recognize their intellectual stance with ease—this of course is even more so now in the current era.

Even if hypothetically the Shīʿa had wanted to hide their actual beliefs now, it would certainly not be an easy feat given that even a cursory web search reveals all their intellectual positions and the locations where they congregate. Thus, what is implied by this constant talk of "the other face of Shīʿism that continues to remain hidden to the Sunnī world?" The time for these banal cliches has vanished and the Shīʿa are now fully uncovered just as others, should anyone spend just a few moments researching their views.

Two Invitations to the Shīʿa and Sunnah Regarding Dissimulation

In this context, we have two pieces of advice to the Sunnī and Shīʿa pertaining to dissimulation:

1. We would like those from Ahl al-Sunnah to properly realize that the Imāmī Shīʿa today are not monolithic; they comprise various schools of thought and independent viewpoints that naturally diverge from one another. These differences are apparent and public for everyone to see and this requires some sensitivity in terms of passing

> judgement on the Shīʿa. Therefore, for example, when an individual emerges on a live broadcast and curses the Mother of the Believers ʿĀʾisha, he should not be deemed a spokesman for all Shīʿa. In the same light, when a Sunnī emerges and does takfīr of the Shīʿa we do not generalize and claim that all Sunnīs do takfīr of us—how could this be when a great number of Sunnī Ṣūfīs also hold similar beliefs to us when it comes to gravesites, for instance? Therefore, it is my obligation to differentiate between a Sunnī Salafī and a Sunnī Ṣūfī. Similarly, the Sunnī ought to distinguish between the various currents of Shīʿa thought and not accuse the entire sect for the transgression of a particular group.

If we could become more wary in practicing this crucial differentiation, it would help tremendously in reducing the sectarian pressures in Muslim countries. Shīʿī or Sunnī conservativism in some parts of Pakistan for instance would not speak for the Shīʿī and Sunnī culture in Lebanon, Egypt, or Morocco for instance.

We call upon the conservatives among the Shīʿa to differentiate between those who have enmity towards the Ahl al-Bayt ﷺ and the Sunnīs. There should not be this conflation whereby it is claimed that every Sunnī hates the Ahl al-Bayt ﷺ; it is essential to distinguish between individuals and currents of thought. We call the Sunnīs towards differentiating also between Shīʿī extremists and takfīrīs and moderate/centrist Shīʿas.

2. We would like the Imāmīs to pay attention to the fact that some individuals among them have not ceased to think that it is beneficial to obfuscate and provide others with incorrect beliefs about them under the pretense of dissimulation. We believe that the era of this practice has been terminated. As an example, what is the reason for us to lie and declare unanimity among the Shīʿa about belief in the immaculate preservation of the Qurʾān while we know for certain that some of our scholars do endorse distortion? What is the reason for us to hide the fact that some of our narrations endorse distortion in the Qurʾān just as is also present in the collection of the Sunnīs? Is this monolithic style still effective, or does it instead portray to other sects that Shīʿa scholars and investigators are dishonest and pulling the wool over their eyes?

Our call is towards honesty—let us call towards honesty with the highest integrity—honesty that does not involve hurtful speech towards others—this is what is demanded of every Shīʿa, Sunnī, and Muslim. It is necessary that we accept each other's intellectual differences in belief, history, and jurisprudence without excommunicating one another solely because of divergence. There should not be any attempts towards civil, social, or political suppression such that an individual is forced to lie or compromise their beliefs to live in harmony.

The responsibility is therefore from both directions, and it is not possible for me to demand one specific sect solve the crisis of dissimulation. Instead, this issue is contingent upon cooperation and if we do not strive towards it, we will not be able to solve this issue. I call towards a spirit of collaboration: while we turn towards the Shīʿa to liberate themselves from the remnants of dissimulation, we also direct an invitation to the Sunnīs to differentiate carefully between criminal behavior and a divergence of opinion. The same also applies for the Shīʿa as we outlined. Perhaps by this method we shall be able to live under the shade of a true pluralism that respects the views of others no matter how unorthodox they seem, as long as we remain under the roof of "There is No God but God and Muḥammad is the Messenger of God."

Religious Rituals (*al-Shaʿāʾir*) and Commemorative Occasions (*al-Munāsabāt al-Dīnīyyah*)

Every community, religion, and sect has its own specific rites of practice unique and peculiar to it. These rites are sometimes embedded more deeply in the psyche of that sect than the beliefs by themselves, and the Imāmī Shīʿa are no exception. The particular practices that distinguish this sect are as follows:

1. Visitation of the gravesites of the Imāms of Ahl al-Bayt عليهم السلام in Madīnah, Karbalāʾ, Najaf, Sāmarrāʾ, Kāẓimīyah, Mashhad, etc.

2. Commemoration of ʿĀshūrāʾ and the martyrdom of the grandson of the Prophet ﷺ, Imām al-Ḥusayn عليه السلام. This takes place between the first and tenth of the month of Muḥarram annually and often extends until the end of Ṣafar.

3. Commemoration of ʿĪd such as ʿĪd al-Ghadīr on the 18th of Dhul Ḥijjah, the birth of Imām Muḥammad al-Mahdī عجل الله فرجه on the 15th of Shaʿbān, and the commemoration of Imām ʿAlī's عليه السلام martyrdom on the 19th and 21st of the Holy Month of Ramaḍān, etc.

One may take it for granted that these rituals and ceremonies should not create a point of contention with other sects, however there are some discordant elements which some seek to criminalize them, the goal being to ostracize the Imāmīs from other Muslims. Unfortunately, even some Imāmīs themselves have contributed towards furthering this goal and in our view have unconsciously damaged the reputation of their sect.

The Shīʿa Rituals and the Question of Polytheism (*al-shirk*)

The first issue that has enjoyed widespread circulation is the issue of idolatry and worship of the Imāms of Ahl al-Bayt 🕮. It is claimed that the Shīʿa confirm through their actions their polytheistic non-tawḥīdī-based viewpoint. This results in other sects feeling that there is a phenomenon of aberrant beliefs within the Islamic purview and results in them alienating themselves from their Shīʿa brethren. This is even though visitation of graves is a widespread practice among the Sunnīs themselves!

We have discussed this issue in detail elsewhere and we do not intend to engage in a full-length discourse about belief here; however as far as we know no Shīʿa claims that we perform visitation of Imām ʿAlī al-Riḍā 🕮 in order to worship him or because he is a god other than God 🕮. The Shīʿa literature instead reflects that this is a recommended religious rite just as the rite of pilgrimage (*al-ḥajj*) or the rite of visiting the Prophet 🕮 (*ziyārah al-rasūl*). The fact that Muslims go each year to Makkah and Madīnah does not imply worship of the Kaʿbah. Rather it reflects a communion with those places on the basis of God's 🕮 command and worship. The books of the Shīʿa in reference to the issue of visitation may certainly be reviewed in this juncture.[101]

Nonetheless, it should be said that there are some actions under the purview of these rituals that have become more pervasive over the past few decades and appear odd to members of other denominations. Among these are prostration in front of the graves and directing supplication to the saints (*al-awliyāʾ*) buried at those sites. We have discussed previously in our citations that the Shīʿa scholars have clarified these issues that at first glance appear as deification: prostration in front of a grave is in fact prostration to God ﷻ in gratitude for allowing his servant the privilege of visitation. In the same token, directing supplication to a given saint is nothing but requesting his intercession with God ﷻ and by no means reflects worship or belief in his divinity.

---

[101] A good reference for more background on this issue is the book "*A New Analysis of Wahhābī Doctrines*" by Ḥujjatul Islām Muḥammad Ḥusayn Ibrāhīmī translated by Dr. Mansoor Limba.

However, we believe as Imāmī scholars such as Āyatullāh Sayyid Ḥusayn Burūjirdī ﵀[102] have espoused that it is necessary to cease from practicing these controversial rites that engender misunderstandings about the Shīʿa; this is especially because there is no authentic religious text that substantiates them, and they are merely traditional phenomena.

Our conviction is that any social, psychological, or ritual practice that creates confusion or suspicion in the minds of other Muslims should be abandoned as long as there are not reliable authentic texts that substantiate them based on the criteria established for ḥadīth

---

[102] Āyatullāh Sayyid Ḥusayn Burūjurdī ﵀ (d. 1380 AH) was among the highest Shīʿa religious authorities (*al-maraji'*) of his time and was extremely dedicated to the cause of intrafaith harmony between Shīʿas and Sunnīs. He was an expert in comparative fiqh and was also recognizing as an authority regarding the jurisprudence of the Sunnīs. Among his famous positions was a discouragement of showing excessive reverence to the shrines of the Ahl al-Bayt ﵈—including kissing, crawling, and doing sujūd in front of them—as he believed this engendered misconceptions in the minds of Sunnīs.

authentication in jurisprudence. May God ﷻ help a person who strives to deflect suspicion from himself.[103]

We echo the same statement to Ahl al-Sunnah: every action or behavior that engenders doubt in its relation with others ought to be abandoned as long as it is not substantiated—based on Sunnī criteria—to be based on authenticated texts.

Are the Ḥusaynī Rituals a Conspiracy Against the Rites of Ḥajj and the Holy Ḥaramayn?

Another issue regarding the Shīʿa rituals is their aggrandizement of them to the extent that other Muslims develop the perception that the Imāmīs view it more important than pilgrimage or desire to rival it. They come to hold a false perception that we deem Karbalāʾ more important than Makkah and Madīnah; or that we go to Madīnah and visit the Ahl al-Bayt عليهم السلام at al-

---

[103] This is a common Arabic idiom and is based on some ḥadīth such as the one found in Shaykh Muḥammad b. al-Ḥasan al-Ḥurr al-ʿĀmilī's *Wasāʾil al-Shīʿa*, Vol. 12, p. 36:

مَن دخل موضعًا من مواضع التُهمة فاتُّهم فلا يلومنّ إلا نفسه

"He who enters an arena of suspicion and is accused should not blame anyone except himself."

Baqī'[104] more than we visit the Prophet ﷺ himself; or that we seek to establish Karbalāʾ and Najaf as the epicenters of Islam in place of Makkah and Madīnah; or that there is an attempt to conspire against Islamic history and wipe out the earliest testaments of Islam. These concepts are propagated by some Muslim elements in order to perpetuate belief that the Shīʿas are not Muslim and that they have their own religion with their own sacred symbols and saints that are deemed greater than those mentioned in the Qurʾān and respected by Muslims at large. In some of the jargon used today, we thus hear the term "the Shīʿa religion" as if to emphasize that the Shīʿa are a different religion other than Islam!

The Shīʿa and Sunnī Entry into a Dangerous Bazar

This is in reality not a simple affair; rather I daresay that some Shīʿa have indeed to some extent entered this domain in order to inculcate these ideas into the Muslim psyche. They dig through the religious tradition and historical sources to find hadith that extol Karbalāʾ over Makkah and Madīnah while trying to

---

[104] Jannah al-Baqīʿ or Baqīʿ al-Gharqad is the oldest cemetery of Madīnah and is the location where the second, fourth, fifth, and sixth Shīʿa Imāms ؈ are buried. It is also purported to be the site where Lady Fāṭimah ؉ is buried. The Shīʿa revere this location highly for religious visitation.

weaken those narrations that favor Makkah over all parts of the world.

This is a domain that the Imāmīs have been familiar with for a long time and a trend that had also been present in the Safavid Era, such as the conception that Imāmah is a pillar that is somehow greater in magnitude than belief in God ﷻ, Tawḥīd, and Prophethood. It is thereby subconsciously deemed that anything which is connected to Imāmah is preeminent over that which is tied to Tawḥīd and Prophethood. As we have discussed numerous times in this memorandum, we do not intend to rouse controversy in belief, history, or jurisprudence. However, if the respected reader would allow me, I would like to explore this issue from a more unconventional angle and addend it with some of my own observations. I believe that the reasons why this phenomenon exists are as follows:

1. For hundreds of years, Shīʿa Muslims have been either prohibited or restricted from the practice of visiting the gravesites as also applies to ʿĀshūrāʾ and other ceremonies. However, they were not prohibited from performing the pilgrimage; it is natural that when one is prohibited from something for years—as was the case with restriction of the rituals during the Baathist Iraqi regime or the Ottoman reign of Syria—there will be a massive importance rendered to them once these areas are

liberated. I believe that this phenomenon has had a dramatic role in the current age in the aggrandizement of how these rites are performed in at least some countries.

2. The sectarian strife that has befallen Muslim countries in the last few years has played an important role in resurrecting sectarian-based shows of force; in this galvanized political atmosphere, every sect therefore seeks to accentuate its points of divergence from other sects and affirm their sectarian identity. It is due to this that these rituals and rites have been lent such a tremendous importance: sometimes to affirm a sense of security and insular self-preservation to the sectarian identity; sometimes due to a hidden urge to demonstrate strength in front of other sects and impose a counter power-balance. This in addition to various other political motives that also preserve this climate in the current situation.

What is the Best Course of Action?

We advocate for a multifaceted approach in tackling this issue:

1. It is necessary to decrease the sectarian pressure in the Muslim region as a preamble to eventually extinguishing it. This is a religious, political, media, and cultural obligation.

2. The endeavoring to separate political agents from the realm of sectarian/religious affairs, and this is the responsibility of Muslim scholars.

3. Cessation or at least reduction of attacks by Ahl al-Sunnah against these rituals because sectarian conflicts in such a high-strung partisan atmosphere will not result in anything except further insistence on these rituals.

4. The effort of Shīʿa scholars to clarify the situation by bringing to the forefront the history of the Holy Prophet ﷺ and the mutually recognized Islamic history. This should also involve dismantling some of the common misconceptions regarding the status of Makkah and Madīnah as well as granting Shīʿa rituals their proper worth away from exaggerations. It is important that they not compromise the shared elements between all Muslims for the sake of particularly Shīʿa practices.

I believe that if we can endeavor together to establish these four elements, misunderstandings would dissipate and this sectarian vulnerability exploited by extremists would vanish. Instead, these rites and practices would be appreciated as manifestations of love for the Prophet ﷺ and his Ahl al-Bayt عليهم السلام. There would be no sense of fear or worry even if millions attend annually; rather this would be seen as a true and honest expression of love for the Ahl al-Bayt of the Prophet ﷺ who are revered by all.

On this note, we also direct an invitation to other Muslims to participate in the commemoration of ʿĀshūrāʾ and visitation of Imām al-Ḥusayn ؑ in Karbalāʾ because Imām al-Ḥusayn ؑ is certainly not just for the Shīʿa. He is a paragon for all Muslims—rather for every person who values liberty and honor. Indeed, based on this paradigm ʿĀshūrāʾ becomes an Islamic issue that exemplifies the proximity among Muslims instead of being an agent of conflict and schism.

What about Specific Rituals such as Self-Flagellation (*al-taṭbīr*) and their Like?

The third issue concerning rituals is the existence of some rites that engender repulsion or suspicion about the Imāmi Shīʿa on the part of most Muslims; these practices include bloodletting (*al-taṭbīr*), walking on coals/fire (*al-mashyu ʿalā al-jamr*), self-flagellation (*ḍarb al-jasad bi al-salāsil*), crawling and groveling like a dog for entry to the gravesites (*al-zaḥf wa al-mashyu mashyat al-kilāb*), self-bondage (*waḍʿ al-aqfāl)*, self-injurious slapping (*al-laṭm al-mudmī*), stripping oneself (*shibh al-taʿarrī*), describing oneself as a dog of the Ahl al-Bayt ؑ(*naʿt al-dhāt bi kalb al-aʾimmah*), and eulogization of the Ahl al-Bayt ؑ in a way that violates their station and contradicts religious beliefs. These phenomena do not have any clear religious texts condoning them and are merely human and cultural expressions of grief and lamentation.

Today they are no longer representative of rejuvenating the commemoration of the Ahl al-Bayt ﷺ; that is, instead of these ceremonies being symbolic of confrontation against sociopolitical oppression and corruption while representing the establishment of justice, revolt, perseverance, martyrdom, and self-determination, they are looked at now in a completely different light. It is time we join the ranks of the Shīʿa and Sunnī voices that continue to call towards the abolishment of these practices and the establishment of a new spirit that embodies proper ritualization and enlightens the hearts, minds, and souls. We therefore rebuke all these practices and call towards reforming these rituals and returning to their traditional iterations of visitation (*al-ziyārah*), crying (*al-bukāʾ*), recounting their tragedies (*al-tadhkīr bi mā jarā ʿalayhim*), love for them (*mawaddah*), and revival of their principles (*iḥyāʾ amrihim*). We deem it the responsibility of the scholars, jurists, religious authorities, and educated folk to enact this change.

The Crisis of Reducing Shīʿīsm (*ikhtizāl al-tashayyuʿ*) to Rituals

Whatever the case, Shīʿīsm ought not to be reduced to only these practices in the eyes of the Muslims at large and even some of the Shīʿa. Rather, Shīʾism has many precepts that ought to be examined before passing judgement on it solely by virtue of its rituals. Shīʾism is rather a history of engagement, bounty, struggle, recognition and love for the Prophet ﷺ and his family, and defense of Islam and Muslims. Shīʾism is what issued forth geniuses, scholars, thinkers, and revolutionaries (especially in the current age) while confronting atheism and Westernization. It has fought and offered martyrs in fighting the enemies of the Muslim community, not least of which have been the oppressive Zionists. Shīʿa scholars were the ones who issued fatwas in Iraq in defense of the Ottoman Empire against its enemies. It is certainly unjust then that one should neglect this reality and only focus on the rituals that some Shīʿa perform. It is inconceivable that one should reduce an expansive and deep-rooted denomination to these notions and thus pass a negative judgement against it.

Temporary Marriage (*al-zawāj al-muʾaqqat*) and al-Mutʿah

There are a plethora of jurisprudential variances between the Imāmīs and the rest of the Muslims; however as the Shīʿa religious source of emulation Āyatullāh Sayyid Ḥusayn Burūjirdī ؒ is reported to have said as per ʿĀyatullāh Jaʿfar Subḥānī: "The differences between the jurists of the different schools of thought between themselves is not less than the differences between the Shīʿa and Ahl al-Sunnah. The principle of juristic variance is not a crime nor a sin which we can hurl at an entire sect. Rather there is no juristic opinion among the Shīʿa except that it matches the opinion of one of the mainstream Sunnī schools of thought, excepting rare circumstances. This is no exaggeration, rather it is the conclusion of Āyatullāh Sayyid Ḥusayn Burūjirdī ؒ himself after his extensive experience in comparative jurisprudence and research on Shaykh Ṭūsī's ؒ "*The Book of Variation*" (*Kitāb al-Khilāf*).

We have already begun to witness an optimistic movement among both sides—Shīʿa and Sunnī—during the 20th century in recognized the achievements of one another in fiqh, sharīʿah, and its concomitants. There is no need to delve into this extensively here. Since jurisprudential variance is a natural situation, it is not needed for us to devote great efforts to analyze the differences. Nonetheless, there are some topics under the umbrella of jurisprudential variances that are unfortunately handled in an unbecoming way and for which we should all strive to rectify, such as the differences in adhān and iqāmah, folding hands in prayer (*al-takattuf*), saying Āmīn in prayers, prayer times, combining prayers, etc. that we will not have the time to cover here.

Proposing the Founding of a Center for Comparative Fiqh

We propose founding a center for comparative jurisprudence that includes jurists of the Shīʿa, Sunnī, Ibāḍī, and other factions through which we can mutually study issues of jurisprudential variance especially in reference to the jurisprudence of current affairs (*fiqh al-mustaḥdathāt*) and new fiqhī questions (*fiqh al-nawāzil*) in order to ascertain fiqhī conclusions that are more mutually agreed upon while allowing us to become more familiar with the differences in our fiqhī methodologies. This will hopefully be an introduction towards the mutual intersection of knowledge and at the very least encourage the exigency of striving seriously in developing Islamic jurisprudence based on mutual cooperation so that its goals may be actualized most perfectly.

However, in this memorandum I would like to select an issue that is connected to the field of ethics and specifically the moral picture that is painted of the Imāmī Shīʿa in the Islamic world. This issue is much more significant than any other jurisprudential difference because it can hamper the relationship between the two sects due to the repulsion that it engenders. This issue is that of temporary marriage (known in Arabic as *al-zawāj al-muʾaqqat*, *nikāḥ al-mutʿah*, and *al-nikāh al-munqaṭiʿ*) and how it is perceived by some in being a legalization of the crime of fornication (*al-zinā*). It is conceived that it is a justification towards moral depravity and promiscuity between men and women and that the Imāmī Shī'a—according to this premise—will be a community that reneges against chastity and renders all their women as sexually licit for all their men, etc.

I do not want to engage here in a jurisprudential-historical debate about whether the Muslims accepted the legality of this form of marriage. The fact is that they differed regarding whether it was abrogated or limited to a very specific temporal situation during wartime. As we all know, this was a quarrel that erupted between the companions and the succeeding generations themselves, and they split into various factions. It is also well-known that the view of the companion 'Abdullāh b. 'Abbās and his entourage was the belief in the permissibility of temporary marriage.

The Imāmī Shī'as—in concordance with the consensus of their Imāms from Ahl al-Bayt 🕊️—also believe in the permissibility of temporary marriage and that it was not abrogated. Rather, they view this form of marriage as a key towards solving a great number of contemporary problems to the extent that even some jurists among the Ahl al-Sunnah have themselves moved toward allowing a form of marriage like it in recent times. Of course, this has been the consequence of severe lifestyle pressures and the difficulties in getting married within the Islamic world and the Muslim community abroad.

Let us be honest and travel to the Shīʿa countries in the East and the West: will we truly find such a deterioration of morality and deviation away from religious principles beyond that found in other Muslim countries? To the contrary: we see that the veil (*al-ḥijāb*) is obligatory, shaking hands and touching (*al-muṣāfaḥah wa al-mass*) the opposite gender is prohibited, lustful glances (*al-naẓar*) are prohibited, etc. The books of the Shīʿa and their religious milieu are a testament to the fact that there is no difference. It is possible for any individual to come forward in any manner and verify for himself the religious adherence among the practicing Shīʿa in following the juristic edicts of their scholars.

What is the Story Behind Temporary Marriage and What is its Sharʿī Form?

It is a form of marriage just as permanent marriage, except with some minor differences. As in permanent marriage, there should be intent (*al-qaṣd*), choice (*al-ikhtiyār*), mutual consent (*al-tarāḍī*), and the other standard qualities between spouses such as not being married to someone else and lack of blood, marriage, or milk kinship. This marriage is also contingent upon all the same prerequisites as permanent marriage such as dowry (*al-mahr*), familial relationships (on the basis of in-law, milk, and blood ties), child-rearing (*al-nafaqah*), inheritance of children (*al-tawāruth*), the necessity of maintaining family bonds (*ṣilah al-raḥim*), etc. It is indeed a complete spousal relationship that is verifiable and holds weight in religious courts.

The only major differences whereby temporary marriage differs from permanent marriage are in the following:

a. It is only valid for a prescribed amount of time.

b. It is not mandatory for the husband to bear his wife's expenses.

c. Separation does not occur by divorce but rather by either expiation of the allotted time or by gifting the remainder of the time to one's spouse (*al-hibah*).

d. The waiting period after the relationship is no more than two menstruations.

e. There is no mutual inheritance between the husband and wife.[105]

---

[105] For more details about mutʿah marriage, one may refer to the excellent work of Dr. Sachiko Murata in her "*Mutʿa: Temporary Marriage in Islamic Law.*"

If we are to examine these aforementioned differences carefully, we realize that they are in complete concordance with the purpose of this marriage: relief of sexual lust in a sharīʿah-compliant manner when one is economically incapable of permanent marriage. Hence, we see that the requirements of expenditure and permanence have been nullified.

The concept behind temporary marriage is not that any man can have a relationship with any woman without legal restriction; rather it implies all the same parameters as permanent marriage while also satisfying temporary exigency. As Islam had legitimized temporary marriage for the companions in the context of severe social pressures, it gives the same concession to other Muslims. Now if some do misappropriate the use of temporary marriage, then by the same token many also take advantage and misappropriate permanent marriage (*al-zawāj al-dā'im*), polygamy (*taʿadud al-zawjāt*), and the male prerogative for divorce (*ḥaqq al-ṭalāq li al-rajul*). The mismanagement of a right does not entail that a human being should be stripped of his established right, otherwise no right could be legitimately established for anyone.

It is from this perspective that we advocate firstly for treating this marriage as a respectable form of juristic practice (*al-ijtihād*), just as is the case with the marriage of misyār[106] for instance; we also call toward ending the circulation of immoral impressions about this form of marriage. Secondly, we encourage its official legal systemization and the abolishment of treating it as a sectarian Shīʿa issue as though it is only borne out of enmity for the second Caliph ʿUmar b. al-Khattab due to his prohibition against it. Rather it should be dealt with as an Islamic law that can serve as a sharīʿah-compliant solution in the present age in the setting of male and female psychological and sexual pressures.

When we can understand this marriage properly while also being cognizant about the limits of its application, instead of seeing it as moral degeneracy we may begin to see the positive aspects it can bring to the table in opposing the widespread collapse of morality. Indeed, Shīʿa fiqh is relatively quite conservative regarding the relationship between men and women as it prohibits ogling (*al-naẓar*), touching (*al-lams*), and shaking hands (*al-muṣāfaḥah*) with the licit (*ghayr maḥram*) from the opposite gender.

106 This is also known as "traveler's marriage" and is accepted by some Sunnīs, especially for couples who are unable to live together or do not want to start a permanent family.

Shīʿa Expansionism (*al-Madd al-Shīʿī*) and Shīʿa Disruption of the Peace in Sunnī Beliefs

This issue has formed one of the flash points in recent years between the Shīʿa and Sunnī denominations. It is often claimed that the Shīʿa strive towards spreading their sect within the Sunnī atmosphere by exploiting the political and military achievements they have actualized over the past three decades. The Sunnī side espouses that the spread of Shīʾism in a Sunnī-majority environment leads to a compromise in their religious integrity and generates socioreligious schisms that negatively impact Islamic society. Sectarian promulgation creates splinters within the social web and is a transgression against the state of well-being existing in Sunnī-majority countries.

The Necessity of Understanding the Sunnī Anxiety about the Spread of Shīʿīsm

In the first place, it is necessary to understand the worry with which some Sunnī scholars live while seeing the pendulum of sectarian integrity swinging to the benefit of the Shīʿa within their societies. I am not at all concerned here in bringing up controversial issues such as whether there is truly an agenda to spread Shīʾism within the Sunnī world, whether this is a state-sponsored or organizational-based initiative, whether this is truly a dangerous threat, or whether it is being unnecessarily aggrandized. This is an extended discussion that is not relevant here; based on my personal observation however, I do acknowledge that there are some Shīʿa groups that are striving to promulgate Shīʾism although I do not think it is as expansive as assumed and is vastly overestimated. Rather, this issue has been aggrandized as part of an operation to create sectarian fear and insecurity. At the same time, it should not be forgotten that the Sunnī side also has its own special ambitions in reference to Shīʿa-majority countries.

Just as many prominent Sunnī personalities and celebrities have converted to Shīʾism, there have also been in recent years many Shīʿa personalities who have embraced Sunnīsm. I also acknowledge that the spread of Shīʾism in a given city may engender worry in that city due to possible exploitation of the Shīʿa converts to further the objectives of foreign state powers and vice versa for Sunnī converts.

What Should be the Form of the Solution?

In consideration of the above, let us endeavor towards reaching the framework for a solution while bearing in mind the following two points:

1. The Right of Every Muslim to Spread His Ideas and the Right of Others to Engage and Critique It

It is the right of every Muslim to invite his brethren to what he deems is guidance and truth in both theoretical and practical affairs. This falls under the purview of the duty to enjoin towards good (*al-amr bi al-maʿrūf*), forbid the evil (*al-nahy ʿan al-munkar*), and call others towards piety and truth (*bayān al-ḥaqq*), etc. This is a right that is established for both Shīʿa and Sunnīs and is subsumed within the Islamic Sharīʿa—rather it is deemed obligatory by it.

Therefore, it is not a crime for a person to invite towards what he deems is the truth especially considering the various theoretical and practical interpretations among Muslims. Rather, doing so is an expression of one's practical beliefs in reference to Islam, theology, and Sharīʿa. It is not a sin; whether it be for a Sunnī in Shīʿa lands, a Shīʿa in Sunnī lands, an Ibādī in Shīʿa lands, an Imāmī Shīʿa in Zaydī Shīʿa lands, etc.

If one should believe that the Shīʿi is incorrect in his theological views, then it should also be understood all the while that the Shīʿi considers himself correct and others wrong. Therefore, it is completely logical that he would call others to the interpretation he deems correct in theology and jurisprudence, just as jurists themselves do amongst each other.

2. The Phenomenon of Discrimination Between Islamic Sects in Daʿwah

It is my right to honestly question—given that honesty and discovery is the key to a solution here: why is it that the Salafist ideology is allowed to propagate within Islamic countries while the spreading of the Imāmī sect is deemed a great offense to Islam and Muslims? The Salafīs are allowed virtually unlimited financial support and are not deemed a theological threat; rather they are seen as a sect with whom there is a mere difference of opinion!

I am speaking here solely on a religious level, although the political dimension is equally as salient. For just as the spread of Shīʾism may be seen as an extension of the political authority of Shīʿa countries, the spread of Salafism may equally be seen as a political extension of certain well-known and recognized Sunnī countries. However, I will not knock on the door of political banter here and will restrict my discussion instead solely to the religious aspect.

In my opinion, there is no explanation for this double standard in the treatment of Salafism vs Imāmī Shīʿīsm except the excommunication (*al-takfīr*) of Shīʿas and belief that the spread of their sect is equivalent to the spread of blasphemy (*al-kufr*) as though they were renegades from the religion (*khārij al-millah*). As we have stated before, the issue of excommunication needs to be solved from its very root, otherwise there is absolutely no benefit to speaking about internal Islamic harmony.

In the spirit of integrity, we therefore call the Sunnī religious institutions to revise their general view and stance about the Shīʿa. When they are considered a legitimate Islamic school of thought like the Māturīdīs, the Muʿtazilīs, the Ashʿarīs, the Salafīs, and the Ṣufīs in ʿaqīdah or like the Ḥanafīs, Shāfiʿīs, Ẓāhirīs, Mālikīs, and Ḥanbalīs in fiqh, then why the discrimination against them in the Sunnī world?! Why is it that when a Ṣufī adopts Salafism this is not considered a disaster, while conversion to Imāmī Shīʾism is considered a huge religious dilemma? Why is it that if someone adopts the Mālikī viewpoint after having been Shāfiʿī in jurisprudence, this is not at all a problem that garners controversy while conversion to the Jaʿfarī school of thought raises eyebrows?

Therefore, it behooves us to be honest with ourselves and work towards treating sects (*al-madhāhib*) as Muslims, even if we may beg to differ with their theological and juristic interpretations. Otherwise, let us not be disingenuous by allowing Shīʿas to enter Makkah and Madīnah on the basis of them being Muslim on the one hand, while we treat them as disbelievers on the other!

If the issue is one of innovation (*al-bidʿah*), then let whoever adopts this logic mention a sect that does not contain absolutely any innovation in the theological and juridical schools of which they are wont to be tolerant! Let us be honest with ourselves and explore our own mentalities transparently. I say this all the same to both Shīʿas and Sunnīs, for there are no solutions other than integrity here.

What Have We Achieved in the Face of the Spread of Atheism (*al-ilḥād*) and Areligious Trends (*al-lādīnī*) In the Ummah?

The most ironic reality out of all this is that we seek to restrict Sunnī proselytization in Shīʿa lands and Shīʿa proselytization in Sunnī lands while we give Western ideologies free reign to propagate! This is despite the unanimity amongst us all that it flies in the face of religious and ethical values (of course, even in this circumstance we would favor intellectual confrontation rather than violence, imprisonment, and surveillance). Indeed, Western culture has engulfed a great percentage of our Muslim youth across the spectrum of Mālikīs, Imāmīs, Ibāḍīs, Zaydīs, Ḥanafīs, Shāfiʿīs, Ḥanbalīs, Salafīs, etc. Meanwhile, our Muslim nations are not taking any serious steps against this to the extent that they are against sectarian currents.

It is the right of each of us to call towards his sect while it is the right of those oppose to debate and logically refute it if it is deemed innovative or deviant.

Religious Discourse: Between Presenting Views and Polemical Language

In accordance with the teachings of the Ahl al-Bayt ﷺ, we ought to differentiate between two styles of religious proselytization for the Imāmīs:

1. Presenting its message in an objective manner that does not offend the sensitivities of others without resorting to any argumentation or disputation. In this circumstance, proselytization is a legitimate right.

2. Presenting its message in a disputative and polemical manner that causes rifts and schism in a society (e.g. building a Shīʿa mosque in a village of only ten converts, imposing upon new Shīʿa converts points of divergence that lead to confrontation with their societies, etc.). This type of proselytization is entirely rejected.

As it is narrated from ʿAqabah on the authority of Imām Jaʿfar al-Ṣādiq ؑ: "Devote your affairs for the sake of God, not for the people. Indeed, what was devoted to God will remain with Him, while what was devoted to people will not ascend to Him. Do not dispute with people about your religion, for disputation renders disease upon the heart (*mumriḍah li al-qalb*)."[107] Similarly there is a hadith on the authority of Abū Baṣīr on the authority of Imām Muḥammad al-Bāqir ﷺ: "Do not dispute with the people, for if they were capable of loving us, they would naturally do so."[108]

The textual sources of the Prophetic household therefore prohibit disputation, rigidity, and excess in proselytization of Shīʾism in a way that would engender animosity. This is categorically reprehensible, even though some Shīʿa today may still engage in it. Of course, we emphasize the exact same principle to those who seek to spread Sunnīsm in Shīʿa lands while sowing the seeds of dispute, hatred, and rancor amidst the populace.

However, why should we deem offensive a person who utilizes an objective and well-balanced approach to guide people to what he deems truth and guidance? Rather, it is more appropriate that we should grant him the right to do so while engaging with him in an objective manner.

---

[107] Kulaynī, Shaykh Muḥammad b. Yaʿqūb, *al-Kāfī*, Vol. 1, p. 166.

Ṣadūq, Shaykh Muḥammad b. ʿAlī, *al-Tawḥīd*, p. 414-415.

[108] al-Barqī, Aḥmad b. Muḥammad b. Khālid, *al-Maḥāsin*, Vol. 1, p. 136 and 203.

Who is Responsible for the Spread of Shīʿīsm in the World?

If it is true that Shīʿīsm is being spread in a way that engenders anxiety—as espoused by some even though there is also spread of Sunnīsm in Shīʿa lands—then this should be deemed a failure of the scholars of the Sunnī religious institutions. Why is it that instead of criticizing the source of this failure, we instead resort to inflammatory sectarian tactics that seek to otherize and ostracize? Is this logical?! If the Sunnī religious institutions endeavored in a proper manner, people would not abandon their sect in such large numbers; therefore, why the efforts to bury this weakness through attacks on others? I believe that this matter is categorically political, and I call for redacting it from circulation in social and religious atmospheres, especially because nearly everyone engages in this phenomenon except the religiously marginalized that seek to protect their own identity and cannot think about disparaging others.

We live during the era of knowledge, plurality, difference of opinion, cultural diffusion, technology and the information explosion; it is no longer possible for us to restrict the beliefs and thoughts of others from exerting their influence in our societies. Our countries are open for whomever wants to spread his/her thoughts and the era of ideological suppression has long been terminated.

Therefore, let us submit to this new reality and allow our ideological battle to follow suit with this new paradigm; let every faction present its views and perspectives about religion and compete in a constructive manner to draw people towards what they deem as the truth. This should be done without hatred, vengeance, provocation, or attempts to split a society or state. As for anyone who raises controversy and causes tension or sedition through the manner of his proselytization, then it is within the right of the society, whether Shīʿa or Sunnī, to deem him culpable and defend themselves from him. Still however, this particular defense should be spearheaded by the legal and judicial federal powers through an independent due process of law, devoid of political and security motives.

Managing Our Differences: Principles, Methods, and Hermeneutics

Introduction

Among the realities that everyone perceives is that Muslims differ among themselves; it appears that there is no feasible means to lift these theological and judicial differences. The question therefore is: What should be the approach? What steps are necessary for us to take to ensure that our differences do not become the bane of our existence? How do we secure at least the minimal extent of cohesion as an illustrious nation among nations while still preserving these irreconcilable points of differentiation?

We had discussed previously the beliefs of the Imāmī sect and presented the points of controversy that the Imāmī sect may engender in its relationship with other sects. After all these preliminary discussions, how do we treat one another in the midst of all our differences? How do we dissolve the mutual misconceptions and concerns we may have? How can we mitigate the controversy latent in the points of contention that we previously discussed?

Our view in this memorandum is that it is obligatory upon us to establish a number of ethical, humanistic, and religious principles that offer us the right to intellectually differ while still preserving our integrity as

Muslims. The principles we espouse below are general in nature, however if we apply them during the course of our respective lives and manage to establish the consensus of Muslims upon them, they would allow us to regulate our differences in a more suitable manner. We will point to the most important juristic and ethical principles within this limited space as follows:

The First Principle: The Legitimacy of Religious Interpretation (*al-ijtihād*) and the Necessity of Acknowledging Alternative Views

We have been instructed by the Qur'ān to reflect upon its verses and chapters and by the Sunnah to reflect upon its corpus. This implies that the Muslim nation must take on the responsibility of religious interpretation of its texts as is borne out when one sees the efforts expended in Qur'ānic commentary (*al-tafsīr*), Qur'ānic sciences (*'ulūm al-Qur'ān*), ḥadīth, fiqh, theology (*al-kalām*), ethics (*al-akhlāq*), etc. Given that the Muslim nation has carried this responsibility, this would naturally entail the emergence of schools of thought, institutions, and seminaries that take upon themselves the burden of this responsibility.

As long as ijtihād is deemed Islamically legitimate, the possibility of a scholar (*al-mujtahid*) committing errors should be acceptable and even expected. Given that scholars, jurists, mufassirs, and muḥaddiths are not infallible like the Holy Apostle ﷺ and are reliant on the limits of the human ʿaql, errors should be deemed unavoidable even if intentions are correct and purposes are well-envisioned. As long as ijtihād is both a right and obligation upon the ummah and mistakes are unavoidable, errors are therefore inevitable.

The logical conclusion from the above is that we should tolerate these mistakes—for anyone who is tasked with a job must acclimate to its conditions. As long as we desire ijtihād to progress, it is upon us as an ummah to accept the natural consequences of opening this door, such as the emergence of mistakes from some mujtahids in assorted subjects.

The Necessity of Opening the Door of Ijtihād in Fiqh, Theology, and History

It is important for us to declare that ijtihād does not stop just at the limits of sharīʿah and fiqh, but rather subsumes theology, tafsīr, historiography, and cosmology; rather it includes everything connected to theology, tawḥīd, prophethood, imāmah, etc.

Of course, there remains one clear red line which is the principle of belief in God ﷻ, His Oneness, and belief in Prophethood and Revelation; as for the details, these are subject to interpretation and we should expect mistakes in the sciences of theology, Qur'ān, Sharīʿa, history, and ḥadīth. It is not necessary or appropriate to consider such error as conspiratorial, disbelief, or stemming from hatred of God ﷻ or His Apostle ﷺ.

When we respect the right of ijtihād and acknowledge it from the depths of our hearts and minds, we will be able to come to an understanding regarding the differences that exist between us. This will become the cornerstone in emerging from deconstructive maligning to constructive criticism, God-willing.

In the realm of the legitimacy of ijtihād, there is therefore no meaning to raising controversy against a certain scholar that he said such and such—this is rather his right. In turn, our right is to discuss and rebut him intellectually through all legal and scholastic means. In the realm of legitimacy of ijtihād, no notion of confrontation, violence, angst, or insulting personalities or schools of thought exists.

How is it possible that someone should acknowledge the freedom and legitimacy of ijtihād while provoking crises whenever scholars emerge with an opinion opposite to his own?! What type of legitimacy and freedom is this? In this formulation it would only imply that "Oh scholars, exercise your right to ijtihād, however beware lest you formulate a view that opposes mine!" This is a nominal fake ijtihād which is sheer emulation and repression.

The Second Principle: Finding Excuses for Other Muslims

When scholars or their followers make a mistake in any issue of ʿaqīdah or fiqh, this does not mean that we should sit idle and not take on the task of guiding through clarification of the truth, invocation of the good, and prohibition of the evil. It is upon every faction among us to reveal his knowledge and face that which he deems a mistake or deviation in the ummah because of incorrect ijtihāds that other groups have adopted. This is a legitimate right for every invoker to God ﷻ who is zealous about his creed; rather it is a religious and divinely sanctioned obligation that was itself the responsibility of the prophets and saints (*al-awliyāʾ*) of God ﷻ throughout history.

However, does confronting a mistake necessitate a criminalization of its committers? Is it the case that because some scholars and their followers made a mistake in some portions of ʿaqīdah or fiqh, they have committed a crime without excuse? Is it not possible that their mistake may garner an excuse in front of the Almighty God ﷻ? The religious principle here is that one ought to "grant to your brother seventy excuses."[109] This rule implies that I ought to seek an excuse for others when they commit mistakes in their ijtihād while endeavoring to correct their error and guide them aright.

Seeking out an excuse for them implies that I should avoid the assumption that they have not earnestly endeavored for the truth and that therefore they have made mistakes; on the contrary, it could very well be that they strived their hardest but still fell short of reaching the reality of the matter.

This methodology is our message: let us come together and differ while each of us practices one's respective right in daʿwah, guidance, and correction. Let us strive to find each other excuses where our views and ijtihāds differ. Let us not impose a connection between error

---

[109] This is a famous Arabic adage, although not a Prophetic narration. In spirit, it finds support in the Qur'ān where God ﷻ says:

﴿يَا أَيُّهَا الَّذِينَ آمَنُوا اجْتَنِبُوا كَثِيرًا مِنَ الظَّنِّ إِنَّ بَعْضَ الظَّنِّ إِثْمٌ﴾

﴾yā-'ayyuhā lladhīna 'āmanū jtanibū kathīran mina ẓ-ẓanni 'inna baʿḍa ẓ-ẓanni 'ithmun﴿

﴾O you who have faith! Avoid much suspicion. Indeed some suspicions are sins.﴿

Sūrat al-Ḥujurāt, Verse 12.

and sin; for it is not necessarily the case that every mistake has emerged from sin or arrogance. Rather, as it is said: "if a mujtahid makes an error he gets a single reward and if he is correct he gets double the reward."[110]

The Third Principle: Convergences and Divergences—No to Disintegrating Sects and No to Disintegrating Islam

In espousing this principle, we mean that there are points of convergence in our views and schools of thought while at other points we diverge. In both cases, it behooves us to shed light on both aspects.

We therefore oppose this notion of only focusing on the points of convergence like the shahādah, ṣalāt, ḥajj, zakāt, jihād, ṣawm, etc. while negating or suppression the points of divergence. It is the right of every sect to declare and defend its viewpoint when it comes to ʿaqīdah, tārīkh, and fiqh while also being offered the chance to critique the views of other schools of thought. We oppose closing the chapter of discussing sectarian variance. However, this does not imply that we should forget the points of similarity between us.

---

[110] This is a ḥadīth narrated in Sunnī books, such as *al-Bukhārī* (ḥadīth n. 6805) and *al-Muslim* (ḥadīth n. 3240).

The Shīʿa and Sunnī equally are encouraged therefore to underscore the points of similarity between them—it is not correct for either to display oneself as being completely different from the other Muslim sects. Most of our primary beliefs and secondary legal edicts are derived from the same sources and it is necessary that we bring this to the fore when managing our differences. Lest our differences become a catalyst to fomenting a culture of otherization, it is necessary for us to set the background by emphasizing our similarities and then discussing our differences upon this backdrop.

Our message in the contemporary age is that we ought to converge and diverge in harmony; our message is that we ought not to cancel out our similarities or differences but rather, we should convene and underscore what we agree upon while also maintaining the unique views that each of us possess in ʿaqīdah and sharīʿah.

We are against the dissolution and cancellation of sects —as this is an unrealistic notion—and we also oppose closing the door of ijtihād and difference in those areas where Muslims differ. We advocate towards the necessity of adopting balanced views that take heed to the points of similarity and difference between us, such that we do not dissolve our divergence as sects while also not dissolving our unity as a religion.

Our reading therefore does not rely upon negation of our individual sects nor our Islamic creed; rather it preserves both. This is a very important point in managing our differences.

The Fourth Principle: Minorities and the Majority—Fostering and Integration

This principle implies that within the Muslim ummah there is a majority (the Sunnīs) and minorities (the Ismāʿīlīs, the Zaydīs, the Ibāḍīs, the Imāmīs, etc.). In turn, each country has a majority and several minorities —sometimes a Shīʿa majority and a Sunnī minority as is the case in Iran and Azerbaijan or vice versa as is the case in the countries of North Africa, Pakistan, Indonesia, Malaysia, etc. Notwithstanding that, we prefer to avoid speaking about Muslims with the language of majority and minorities, as we are all one. The question that arises here then is as follows:

What is the religious principle that ought to govern the relationships of the minorities with the majority and vice versa within the Islamic superstructure? We view it as a twin pair of principles: fostering (*al-iḥtiḍān*) and integration (*al-indimāj*)

1. The fostering of the minorities by the majority through welcoming them, respecting them, opening the society for them, and offering them the freedom for their self-preservation while considered them a

national preserve in the spirit of diversity and harmonious living. They should be granted their legal rights in employment, legal proceedings, media, freedom of speech, etc.

2. The integration of the minorities into the majority, meaning that they should not seek to be insular and recalcitrant in their environment. Rather they ought to seek to cooperate and establish a national and religious identity without feeling like they are reliving the tensions of bygone history with the majority faction among which they live.

These principles of fostering and integration also imply foregoing dissension and the sowing of contention with others. We observe that this principle is a joint duty and is not possible to actualize without cooperation from both parties. Unilateral steps do not avail except in a very limited manner. Therefore, we call for integration that demands from minorities that they should liberate themselves from ostracization, insulation, and historical trepidation while demanding from the majority that they forego the logic of dominance and monopolization; to the extent that these steps are mutually implemented, this endeavor will succeed.

The Citizenship of the Shīʿa in the Arab World

Among the issues that contentiously come up within the Arab world is the question of the relationship of the

Shīʿa to non-Arab foreign influences—specifically to Persian Iran and non-Arab religious leadership. Every Arab Shīʿa is thus accused of being an Iranian citizen whose allegiances are to Iran and not to the respective Arab nation. He is accused of being affiliated to foreign religious authorities that restrict his patriotism. This accusation against a Shīʿī is then taken as a pretext to call into question his citizenship. I do not want to engage in a long discussion here about the various iterations of Arab Shīʿa across the span of history; what pertains to us is two points:

1. Religious affiliation with jurisprudential authorities that live outside the confines of a given state does not violate one's citizenship. This is especially the case when we consider the fact that these same religious authorities mostly call upon their followers to adhere to the laws of the respective land where they take residence; by no means is anyone summoned to not defend his homeland nor defy, surrender, or betray it.

On a similar vein, the religious affiliation of the Catholic Christians ties them to the Vatican while many of the Sunnīs tie themselves to al-Azhar or Saudi Arabia while not impeding on their citizenship in Libya, Sudan, Yemen, Syria, Algeria, etc. One can observe the same when it comes to non-Arab Muslim countries such as Malaysia, Bangladesh, Pakistan, India, etc. whereby their affiliation with Arab religious authorities does not renege their citizenship and patriotism to their countries. The same principle ought to apply to the Imāmī Shīʿa when he adheres to his religious authority in Iraq and Iran in reference to his Islamic obligations; therefore, why is only this relationship seen as violating the legitimacy of his citizenship?!

How come is it that the hundreds of millions of Sunnīs in both East and West Asia who adhere to the edicts of scholars in Egypt, Saudi Arabia, or Qatar are not deemed in violation of their citizenship to their country meanwhile the Arab Shīʿa, who follow a religious authority in Iraq who expresses no animosity or negative stance towards Arabs, are deemed a dilemma? Of course, if people were rational and objective, perhaps they would not see any dilemma at all in such issues.

2. Let us leave the issue of religious authorities and discuss concerning foreign powers; it behooves us to ask the majority within Arab countries a simple question: why do you think the Arab Shīʿa resort to the shelter of Iran as you say while the majority of their religious authorities reside in Iraq? Does this not tell us that they are estranged from a warm embrace within the Arab world?

In an environment where sectarian discrimination is carried out against a Shīʿī such that he feels he is constantly being spied upon and targeted while being restricted in his employment and religious freedoms, it is natural for him to seek out a refuge that grants him security and confidence. When he is constantly being told that he is not wanted and that he is a second-class citizen, this should not at all come as strange. This same issue in fact takes place in countries that consist of Shīʿa majority when its government employs these same politics; you will find those Sunnīs who affiliate themselves to Saudi Arabia also facing the same conundrum.

How is it fair that we place the responsibility of this situation on the shoulders of the victims while exculpating the hegemonic policies in such Muslim nations?! Every time we raise the roof of sectarianism and religious discrimination in Arab societies, we will be imposing forcefully on the Arab Shīʿa to resort to their strategic last resorts such as Iran.

I do not wish here to discuss Iran and the nature of its operations, as this is not the point of our discussion. Rather I only seek to shed light on the reasons for the situation that we deem pressing in relation to citizenship and nationalism.

For example, if we were to do the same to the Christians in the Arab world, it would be only natural for them to turn to the West to seek repose; the same applies for any other minority. Therefore, instead of blaming minorities it is more appropriate to blame ourselves who reside in the Arab world. Indeed, what have we—the wealthy, privileged, and entitled of the Arab world—done to foster these minorities by guaranteeing their safety and rights?!

It is indeed strange that our Arab countries instead accuse the leaders of these disenfranchised minorities and turn a blind eye to their own negligence in including them as citizenry. At the same time, Iran is blamed even though it has for many decades been able to foster refuge for many among the Arab Sunnīs! How did Shīʿa Iran succeed in attracting the Arab Sunnīs who are not even native to its terrain, while Arab countries have failed to that with their own native Arab Shīʿa—and even some Sunnī—populations?!

This is indeed among the marvels of our Arab nation and the self-interested policies of its rulers, whereby they seek to find the solution in a place other than the source from whence it emerged. As we have stated before, the issue of citizenship cannot be solved without the paradigm of fostering and integration.

The Fifth Principle: The Basis of Liberty and Security

It is not possible for us to establish our variance on solid ground if we do not believe in the principle of liberty in

Islam; liberty in this context does not at all imply recalcitrance against the Sharīʿah or exercising unethical behavior. Liberty here refers to the natural product of the first four principles we previously espoused; more specifically it refers to freedom in the following domains:

a. the freedom to express one's religious identity,

b. the freedom to practice one's religious rites with safety and peace

c. opening the door for free participation in political, social, and economic life

d. freedom in general and private forms of media and broadcasting

e. freedom to critique

f. freedom of belief in concordance with ijtihad under the banner of monotheism and prophethood

g. freedom of work, domicile, and transportation while lifting all forms of discrimination against minorities

h. freedom to build religious establishments and furnish them both from a materialistic and spiritual standpoint in a way that preserves social balance and peaceful living.

The appeal is firstly to the clergymen to assure these freedoms by providing the religious framework; secondly, it is to the politicians and journalists to provide the infrastructure for these provisions. Thirdly and more generally, this appeal is leveled to all of society to accept this guiding ideal. It is the role of scholars, aristocrats, and reporters to promulgate this culture of **responsible** liberty rather than a notion of **unfettered** liberty—a productive and conscientious liberty and not the kind that leads to self-indulgence or admittance into Hellfire.

The Sixth Principle: Separating Religious (*al-madhhabī*) and Political (*al-siyāsī*)

By this we do not mean secularism, but rather we mean to say that media correspondents, clergy, and aristocrats must work in tandem to separate between the dimensions of religion and political interests. It should not be the case that the Imāmī Shīʿa are politically stigmatized with this idea of being agents, nor vice versa for the Sunnīs or minorities like the Zaydīs or Ibāḍīs.

Herein lies the role of media and clergy to ensure that government bodies and political parties are not reduced to sectarian agendas and that there is preservation of every individual's political right and opinion. We call upon the Shīʿa and Sunnīs equally to support the religious governments wherein they see an element of strength for the Muslims against their adversaries. However, at the same time we refute the efforts of some countries and political organizations to sectarianize, as the sects of Islam truly transcend any political motives.

Our message is that a Sunnī should not be oppressed because one happens for instance to be against a certain Sunnī country; we should not violate the rights of a Shīʿī because we are against a certain Shīʿa country. Let us liberate religion and sects from politicians; while secularism calls for separation between religion and politics as well, what we advocate for is a separation while preserving ethical and religious values within politics. Among the Shīʿa are those against a Shīʿa government and among the Sunnīs are those who are against a Sunnī government; these are political factions and our responsibility today is to keep them within their political framework without allowing politicians to take advantage of religious sentiments to achieve their own interests.

What are the Necessary Steps to Take?

Practical Steps are Essential

We discussed previously regarding the definition of the Twelver Shīʿī Imāmī sect, known from a fiqhi standpoint as the Jaʿfarī school of thought; then we discussed the controversial issues that exist between the Sunnīs and the Imāmīs; finally, we discussed rules that may govern management of our differences. Now we would like to outline—In our usual brief style—the practical steps we ought to pursue and we have divided them as follows:

Reviewing Our Sects with a Critical Eye (Refining the Religious Corpus)

This ought to be done without bias or excessiveness; what is deemed untenable ought to be cast aside and repudiated. We ought to have the audacity to perform this while keeping God ﷻ alone in mind. In this vein, we must reject the notion of an infallible sect, as no such thing exists. Even though the Prophet ﷺ, companions, and the Ahl al-Bayt عليهم السلام may or may not be considered infallible, the fact is that both Shīʿa and Sunnah commit mistakes; and indeed, acknowledging these mistakes is meritorious.

It is similarly necessary to refine the ḥadīth corpus of all sectarian agendas and to critique them intellectually; by this we do not advocate for fabrication or manipulation of religious literature. Rather, what is implied is that the historical and fiqhi ḥadīth corpus that we deem as part of the public heritage needs to be worked upon and refined to present the correct and substantiated portions therein. As for the texts that malign the Prophet's ﷺ image or represent extremist tendencies, it is upon the scholars to flag these and point out that they do not represent the official school of thought but rather are fringe views adopted by some.

Reviewing Our Reading of Other Sects

Another goal should be for us to adopt an objective understanding about other sects through reliance on the principles we previously discussed, rather than a sectarian or polemical one: objective study of other schools of thought stripped from the logic of debate and egotism and buttressed with the logic of intellectual collaboration to reach a more seasoned and cultured view. This is a necessary step to extricate ourselves from the crisis in which we find ourselves.

Striving Towards Showing the High Points of Other Sects

In order to extinguish the pessimistic situation in which we find ourselves so that we cease to live our lives while perpetrating only the weakest aspects of other schools of thought, it is necessary for us to begin to look with eyes of optimism at others. We should see their strengths and acknowledge them while critiquing their points of weakness with the aim of promoting reform and improvement. In turn, our opposition should practice the same policy with us such that he should critique what he views as errors in our thought with objectivity, intellectual honesty, and respect while also acknowledging our points of strength. When religious institutions and the general social psyche is ready for this type of discourse, we will then be at the cusp of a new horizon.

Extending Bridges for Mutual Collaboration between Schools of Thought

This should be accomplished by regular mutual visits between scholars and seminarians in Iraq, Iran, Bahrain, Lebanon, Egypt, Saudi Arabia, Malaysia, Oman, Yemen, Algeria, Morocco, etc. The goal of this endeavor should be establishing mutual acquaintances while breaking down barriers and misunderstandings.

It is important for these bridges of communication to not be established on excessively formalized and pretentious protocols. Rather, we ought to discuss the root issues that create anxiety and tension with one another to relinquish these misunderstandings and envision solutions. To this end, it is necessary to eliminate the language of opacity and dissimulation, as this type of language obstructs the cooperation between sects, leading to lies and stratagems that can completely dismantle the basis of a true partnership.

Establishing Positions in Universities and Seminaries for Cross-Sectarian Studies

This should be a common goal among all sects. There should be specific appointments agreed upon between religious institutions to send students as deputies to a number of different institutions. Sunnī, Zaydī, and Ibāḍī delegations should be sent to Shīʿa Imāmī institutions in Qum and Najaf. Meanwhile, the Shīʿa Imāmī should send their delegations to the Sunnī establishments of al-Azhar, Morocco, and Oman.

The Immediate Cessation of Offensive Sectarian Propaganda

This is especially pertinent to satellite channels that promote programs and speakers that seek to stir up discord. Manuscripts, books, and media disseminations that promote hatred and animosity must be dismantled under the pretext of their criminality for spreading disharmony among Muslims, catalyzing the shedding of their blood, and violating their honor and property rights. Muslim governments and authorities must unite in condemning and terminating these continued theatrics.

It is necessary that we establish our religious discourse on an intellectual basis and not one of contention and polemics. As we have stated before, each school of thought has its points of weakness and obsessing over this alone will not yield anything but an unsavory stigmatism.

Media plays a fundamental role in establishing this partnership and should employ directed strategic steps through conscientious programs, especially for children and adolescents, that nurture a generation built on mutual understanding, respect, and tolerance. Literature and art have a role in this in what they present of stories, poetry, religious melodies, theatricals, and television series; it is important for us not to belittle this important responsibility that also subsumes these disciplines.

Benefiting from the Experiences of Religiously Tolerant Countries

This is especially in reference to countries that have enjoyed an environment of tolerance for an extended period of time such as Oman, Sudan, Lebanon, etc. Through studying the experiences of these countries with an inquisitive spirit and enumerating the causes that have led to their short-term and long-term success, it is possible that this may help in identifying important factors to actualize our vision.

This goal should not depend solely on examining Islamic countries, rather it is also possible to derive useful clues from studying non-Muslim societies that have also experienced sectarian and racial strife and division but still emerged victorious, such as North Ireland.

We should also leverage the experience and lessons garnered by previous generations in promoting Muslim unity, such as the Egyptian Dār al-Taqrīb, the Iranian Majmaʿ al-Taqrīb, Islamic unity week, Quds Liberation Day, etc.

Freeing the Clergy by Separating Religion from Politics

By this we mean freeing up the clergy as much as possible from political interests and influences to preserve the integrity of both religion and politics. This requires difficult work in revisioning the relationship between political and religious authority in the Islamic and Arab worlds and striving to offer more independence for the clergy and religious institutions from political decisions and stances. This type of independence for religious authorities is a dire need, as is the necessity for judicial authorities to maintain objective self-sovereignty.

Aligning Political Issues with Religious Issues on Mutual Interests

I mean to say that political and religious endeavors should meet in the common interests and affairs shared by the society, such as the occupation of Palestine, which ought to remain a central issue in the Muslim and Arab world. As such, any country which is governed by a Muslim government, should they be Sunnī or Shīʿa, ought to be seen as a source of power for Muslims. It is necessary for all to recognize the machinations that are being hatched against the entire Muslim world in various forms, especially in the current forms of soft war.

The Necessity to Review the Programs and Priorities of Religious Institutions

It is necessary for religious institutions to turn their attention away from sectarian strife and—in the spirit of preserving our Muslim youth—direct them instead to the currents of atheism and immorality in its plethora of iterations. In turn, it is necessary for them to intellectually engage with the factors that have led to backwardness and stagnation within the Muslim civilization. It is necessary for them to endeavor together on establishing the Qur'ān as the basis for their approaches, being as how it is the foremost commonality between all Muslims.

The priorities today should therefore be focused on the notions of harmonious living, citizenship, partnership, political pluralism, extinguishing the hegemony of monopolization and injustice, fair distribution of power, combating poverty and hunger, establishing legitimate rights and freedoms, and enlivening the energy of religious, humanitarian, and philanthropic institutions. Additionally, there should be a focus on children, women, youth, violence, sex, discourse, acknowledgement, fair distribution of money, elimination of illiteracy, and breaking down socioeconomic inequality.

Our call is towards knowledge, progress, respect for others, time management, employment, cleanliness, organization, adhering to the law, social norms, preserving the moral fabric of society, elevated forms of art, love, hope, etc.

Instead of allowing ourselves and our religious institutions to remain imprisoned in the unceasing dungeons of history and polemics, it is upon us to rise forth with our ummah and re-establish our priorities so that the religious crème-de-la-crème of our society and associated institutions become a productive element of society rather than themselves becoming the source of crises.

To this end, the imperative towards reforming our religious institutions, seminaries, and universities across the entire spectrum of sects becomes obvious. It is important for us to establish transparent programs for nurturing the new generation and training the next speakers, imāms, and missionaries based on the exigencies of the time and priorities of the ummah. The goal of all this is to present a religious discourse that elevates us towards more consequential and substantive goals rather than continued sectarian divisiveness.

Unifying the Efforts of the Moderates of All Sects Against the Fringe Elements

I mean to say that it is necessary for religious institutions, movements, and personalities of all sects to unite in combating extremism within their respective schools of thought. It is necessary for them to formulate practical steps that dismantle the contributing factors towards extremist ideologies within Muslim societies. At the same token, it is necessary to dry out the streams of sectarian hatred by establishing a paradigm for tolerance, love, mutual respect/cooperation, and unification among the Muslims; this aim may be achieved by consolidating all the texts within the Islamic corpus that encourage mutual tolerance and presenting this work to the general Muslim psyche.

Establishing Innovative and Intensive Strategies for Actualizing Mutual Religious Projects

This may be achieved through establishing institutions directed at recording all the shared ḥadīth between the various Muslim sects and promoting intrasectarian comparative fiqh and theology lessons in universities and religious institutions. Councils for nurturing and education should strive to present texts that promote a tolerant psychology and a positive outlook of others in the educational courses they promote whether in the realm of history, philosophy, religions, geography, etc. At the same time, there should be a consolidation of the efforts to combat the phenomena of underdevelopment in the ummah, machinations of its foes, and civility and moral values. This may be accomplished through fostering collaborative organizations and satellite channels that treat the negative issues plaguing the ummah on social, ethical, and educational levels.

We suggest the formation of centers that unite different sects to mutually study and solve the common issues plaguing Arab and Muslim countries. Just as countries have united to designate agreements about international security and cooperation against terrorism, there ought to be similar efforts between sects to come together and confront the ethical decadence plaguing the ummah.

Foregoing Excessive Protocolization in Cross-Sectarian Projects

This implies that truly sincere believers ought to assume the reins of these projects to provide political sanction for them without allowing them to become tools in the hands of politicians.

There has been excessive embellishment in the form and style of unifying sects and this issue is too extensive to cover here. However, it is necessary to elect individuals who are truly invested in efforts for unity so that they could take these projects in their own hands and allow them to flourish into productive results for the ummah.

It is inconceivable that these projects should be managed by a single school of thought, as such an endeavor is doomed to immediate failure. The prerequisite is that they should be managed by the constituents of all sects in order that they may reach a true unification and partnership, God-willing.

The Issuing of Fatwas from Religious Authorities and Foundations to Signify the New Paradigm

The issuance of clear and bold fatwas from religious authorities and institutions is essential to lay the groundwork for this new relationship between the sects. Fatwas have not ceased to carry a great deal of clout in influencing the public even if their influence has diminished within some regions of the Islamic world.

Advocation of Islamic Languages Other than Arabic

These would include languages like Persian, Urdu, Kurdish, Azeri, Turkish, etc. such that it should galvanize us to recognize the cultural heritage of one another in a way that unifies diverse peoples. This is the responsibility of universities, religious institutions, and language schools.

Of course, there are other goals and propositions we could suggest although the nature of this memorandum limits extended discussion. In the past, I have written extensively about the issue of unification within my humble works.

www.ingramcontent.com/pod-product-compliance
Lightning Source LLC
Chambersburg PA
CBHW031502120626
46545CB00005B/1709